Am I Going To Heaven?

A Short Bible Summary of God's Plan
on How to Get to Heaven in Simple Language

Ron Wise
with Helen Atchley

D1004547

xulon
PRESS

To Sarah,

May God always keep
you in His care.

Helen Atchley

Ron Wead

CONTENTS

DEDICATION AND PRAYER

I dedicate this book to my Lord and Savior Jesus Christ. I will leave this book in His hands to reach those whom He wishes to read it.

My hope is that my Lord will bless the marketing group and give them wisdom to come up with creative marketing ideas to get this book into the hands of as many people as possible so they can know God's plan on how to get to heaven.

I pray that the Holy Spirit will convict those who haven't yet accepted Jesus as their Savior. I hope by the time they finish reading this book they will understand all that Jesus went through for them so they could enter His kingdom.

ACKNOWLEDGMENTS

We would like to thank our spouses, Debbie Wise and Bob Atchley, for their patience and encouragement while we were writing this book. We would also like to thank the following people for taking the time to proofread the manuscript and make comments, which played a role in the outcome of the book.

Jo Ann Bailey

Ron and Patti Bradshaw

Debra Burgin

Bill and Georgia Davis

Theo Dues

Tom LaHue

Randy and Joyce Mlinek

Rebekah Mlinek

Stan and Bonnie Whitaker

We are so grateful to have such good friends and family in our lives, people who would take the time and use their gifts to help us in our adventure of writing this book.

THE PLAN

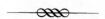

Before you start reading this book, I ask that you have an open mind and also an open heart. Let God speak to your heart. God's words are used in this book, and He tells us that His words will not come back empty but will do the work He intends for them to do. So be prepared to have a different outlook on life at the end of this book.

Before God created the world, He had a plan. His plan was to create people to be happy with Him in heaven. But He knew our limitations, and so He provided for us. He gave us a book called the Bible for us to use as an instruction manual for life. In this book He told us of His plan to bring us to heaven. By inspiring its writers, God wanted us to know that, though we can't get to heaven on our own, He would provide what was needed for us to get there. The Bible is His way of sharing His thoughts with us, and it is written so you may *know* you have eternal life.

1 John 5:11-13 (NLT) "And this is what God has testified: He has given us eternal life, and this life is in his Son. Whoever has the Son has life...I have written this to you who believe in the name of the Son of God, so that you may know you have eternal life."

God created the earth in seven days and has been working on heaven ever since. He wants us to be with Him in heaven and to see the glorious kingdom He has prepared for us. Heaven is a wonderful place—a place with no pain or sadness or sin. Sin is not allowed in heaven. That is what God intended for us from the very beginning of creation.

God used different people to fulfill His plan. This book shows how these people obeyed God and were then blessed by Him. You will learn how God used Noah, Abraham, Isaac, Jacob, Moses, and David (who became king of Israel) to develop His plan.

ETERNAL LIFE

Did you know that each of us will never die? There are only two places created for our eternal life—heaven and hell. We will end up in one of these two places, and we will live there forever.

Originally God intended for us to remain alive forever. That is, we weren't supposed to even die physically. But when sin entered the world, so did punishment and deterioration. Then the pain and anguish began.

We now have to deal constantly with good vs. evil. The book of Revelation tells us there was war in heaven. Michael and his angels fought against the dragon and his angels. The dragon lost the battle, and he and his angels were forced out of heaven. This great dragon—the ancient serpent called the devil, or Satan, the one deceiving the whole world—was thrown down to the earth with all his angels (Rev. 12:7-9). The devil is roaming around the earth looking for anyone he can destroy. The evil one (Satan) wants us all to be miserable with him in hell instead of being happy with God in heaven.

Satan is very good at tricking people. He can change words ever so slightly to fool you. He is a master at putting doubt in our minds, making us unsure of what is right. That is why we need to know God's words well enough to keep us from being tricked. This is also why God gave us the Bible—His Word.

SOMETHING TO THINK ABOUT

Every day people think and dream about what sort of things they would like to do when they retire. Most people do more than just think about it, they actually plan for it. Even after you do all that planning, you still may not live long enough to enjoy it. We don't know how much time God has allowed for us in this life, so we should be preparing for our eternal destination as well.

When we die we will stand before God the Father to face judgment for the way we lived our life here on this earth. Hebrews 9:27 (NLT) says, "And just as each person is destined to die once and after that comes judgment...." So as we are planning for our retirement in this life, how much more should we be looking into where we will spend our eternal life?

Jesus said in Matthew 7:13-14 (NLT), "You can enter God's kingdom only through the narrow gate. The highway to hell is broad, and its gate is wide for the many who choose the easy way. But the gateway to life is small, and the road is narrow, and only a few ever find it." I would like you to be one of the few who finds the right path. Most people think there are a lot of paths that lead to heaven, but Jesus clearly claims otherwise. Jesus said in John 14:6 (NLT), "I am the way, the truth, and the life. No one can come to the Father except through me." Now, if this is true, then there is only one way to enter heaven and not several different paths.

Heaven is so precious that Jesus tells us two parables about it in Matthew 13:44-46 (NIV): "The kingdom of heaven is like treasure hidden in a field. When a man found it, he hid it again, and then in his joy went and sold all he had and bought that field. Again, the kingdom of heaven is like a merchant looking for fine pearls. When he found one of great value, he went away and sold everything he had and bought it."

Jesus is telling us about heaven in a way that we can understand. In 1 Corinthians 2:9 (NLT), Paul says of heaven that "no eye has seen, no ear has heard, and no mind has imagined what God has prepared for those who love him."

Getting into heaven is so important that you need to search the Bible for yourself so that you will know the love God has for you and what He was willing to do to save you from your sins.

Jesus also tells us in Revelation that when we die we will stand in front of a throne and the books will be opened. The word *books* is plural, meaning more than one book. There is the Book of Judgment which records all your deeds, and you will be judged by them. Those who do not profess faith in Jesus will be condemned to hell because their deeds cannot save them. There is also the Book of Life which records the names of those who have accepted God's Son, Jesus, as their Savior. They will be shown mercy and be able to enter heaven for believing in God's Son.

So who is this Jesus and why does He need to save us? In order to find out, we need to start at the very beginning.

GOD CREATES THE WORLD
Genesis 1-3

W hen God created the earth, He created a perfect place called the Garden of Eden. God planted all sorts of trees that grew up from the ground—trees that were beautiful and produced all kinds of delicious fruit. In the middle of the garden He planted the tree of life and the tree of the knowledge of good and evil. Eden had a river flowing through it which kept the garden watered.

Then God created man (Adam) in His own image and placed him in the garden to take care of it. In Matthew 3:9, John said God could have created people out of stones that would be perfect and would obey His commands (like robots), but He wanted people who are willing to choose Him as their King (ruler). So God gave Adam a free will to choose whether to obey Him or not. But God warned Adam, "You may freely eat any fruit in the garden except fruit from the tree of the knowledge of good and evil. If you eat of its fruit, you will surely die."

Then God said, "It's not good for the man to be alone. I will make a helper suitable for him." So God put Adam in a deep sleep and removed one of his ribs and closed the opening. God made a woman from the rib and brought her to Adam, and he was pleased. Adam called her Eve, because she would be the mother of all who live.

We are told in Genesis that the serpent (the devil, Satan) was the shrewdest of all the wild animals God had made. One day the serpent asked the woman, "Did God really say you must not eat the fruit from any of the trees in the garden?"

"Of course we may eat fruit from the trees in the garden," the woman replied. "It's only the fruit from the tree in the middle of the garden that we are not allowed to eat. God said, 'You must not eat it or even touch it; if you do, you will die.'"

"You won't die!" the serpent replied to the woman. "God knows that your eyes will be opened as soon as you eat it, and you will be like God, knowing both good and evil."

The woman was convinced. She saw that the tree was beautiful and its fruit looked delicious, and she wanted the wisdom it would give her. So she took some of the fruit and ate it. Then she gave some to Adam.

Now Adam had a choice to make—whether to obey God's command not to eat from that tree or to go right ahead and eat the forbidden fruit. Adam chose to eat the forbidden fruit. At that moment, sin entered the world through Adam's disobedience to God's command. The sin of this one man, Adam, brought death to mankind through his sin. Not only did his sin bring physical death, but also spiritual death to everyone. Since everyone inherited this sinful nature from Adam, and no one can enter heaven with even one sin on their soul, all people were now going to hell (a place of punishment for those that can't enter heaven).

God knew Adam would sin, and He also knew He wanted to provide a way for us to be saved from hell. Best of all, He knew just how He was going to do it—by sending His Son (Jesus) to the earth to fix the problem.

The moment Adam and Eve ate from the forbidden tree their eyes were opened. They suddenly felt shame at their nakedness. They sewed fig leaves together to cover themselves. They heard the sound of God as He was walking about in the garden, so they hid themselves among the trees. God called to the man, "Where are you?"

Adam replied, "I heard you walking around in the garden, so I hid. I was afraid because I was naked."

"Who told you that you were naked?" God asked. "Have you eaten from the tree whose fruit I commanded you not to eat?"

The man replied, "The woman you put here with me—she gave me some fruit from the tree and I ate it."

Then God asked the woman, "What is this you have done?"

"The serpent deceived me and I ate it," she replied.

Because of God's righteousness, sin cannot go unpunished. So God punished the serpent and said, "Because you have done this, cursed are you above all the livestock and all the wild animals! You will crawl on your belly and you will eat dust all the days of your life. And I will put enmity between you and the woman, and between your offspring and hers; he will crush your head, and you will strike his heel." So there will always be two types of people in this world—the godly and the ungodly—and they will always be fighting among themselves.

God also punished the woman and told her, "I will greatly increase your pains in childbearing; with pain you will give birth to children. Your desire will be for your husband, and he will rule over you."

God also punished Adam. He said, "Cursed is the ground because of you; through painful toil you will eat of it all the days of your life. It will produce thorns and thistles for you, and you will eat the plants of the field. By the sweat of your brow you will eat your food until you return to the ground, since from it you were taken; for dust you are and to dust you will return."

Then God made clothes for them out of animal skin. He caused blood to be shed by an animal in order to cover their nakedness, and blood represents life. For Leviticus 17:11 (NLT) says "the life of the body is in its blood."

God said, "The man has now become like one of us, knowing good and evil. He must not be allowed to reach out his hand and take also from the tree of life and eat, and live forever." So God banished Adam from the Garden of Eden, and he sent Adam out to cultivate the ground from which he had been made.

Now, because of their disobedience, they were kicked out of the Garden of Eden and were not allowed to return. They had to live in the world in which we live today.

Adam had a free will. He chose to disobey God by eating the forbidden fruit, which brought sin into the world. God knew from the beginning that man would be tempted and not be able to go through this life without sinning. In His foreknowledge, He provided a "way" for us to be able to spend our eternal life with Him in heaven where He prepares a place for those who love Him. 1 Peter 1:20 says God chose His Son, Jesus, to be our "way" for this purpose long before the world began. Jesus is our Savior—saving us from hell.

ATONEMENT FOR SINS

G od shed the blood of animals to clothe Adam and Eve's nakedness. The shedding of blood took place because of their disobedience. In the same way that bloodshed was needed to cover their nakedness, it now is needed to remove our sinfulness. God chose the shedding of blood to cover our sins. Hebrews 9:22 says that without the shedding of blood there is no forgiveness.

Animal blood is not the way God had intended to remove human sins, but He did provide a way for the sins of the people to be forgiven. In Leviticus chapter 4 God set up a priesthood, and one of the duties of the high priest was to once a year (on the Day of Atonement) go behind the curtain in the temple to offer sacrifices for his sins and the sins of the people of Israel. Each year this sacrifice would push back their sin debt until the next year. Perfect unblemished animals needed to be used for these sacrifices. The high priest had to do this year after year until the time came when God would provide a proper sacrifice for sin once and for all. In order for sin to be completely and permanently forgiven, a perfect sinless person would have to shed his blood as a sacrifice. (God's plan was to send His Son, Jesus, to be that proper sacrifice.)

In Exodus 26:1-3 God gave special instructions on how this curtain was to be made. This special curtain was very thick and very well made. It separated the Holy Place from the Most Holy Place, the sacred area that only the high priest could enter once a year to offer a sacrifice for the people of Israel to cover their sins, and his, for another year.

The sacrifices under the old system were repeated again and again, year after year, but they were never able to provide perfect cleansing for those who came to worship. If they could have provided perfect cleansing, the sacrifices would have stopped because the worshipers would have been purified for all time and their feelings of guilt would have disappeared. But just the opposite happened. Those yearly sacrifices reminded them of their sins year after year.

As the people started to multiply on the earth, they became more and more wicked. The Lord saw that everything they thought and did was totally evil. It broke His heart. He was sorry He made them and said, "I will wipe mankind, whom I created, from the face of the earth...for I am grieved that I have made them" (Gen. 6:6-7 NIV).

NOAH FINDS FAVOR WITH GOD

Genesis 6-9

God was going to destroy all of mankind. But Noah found favor in the eyes of the Lord. God told Noah to build a large boat (the ark). God gave Noah directions on how to build it and what He wanted him to put on the boat when he finished it.

Noah got into the ark with his wife, his three sons, and their wives—a total of eight persons in all. Because of Noah's righteousness and his love for God, God spared his life and the lives of his family from the flood that came on the earth.

After the flood, God told Noah and his sons, "This is the sign of the covenant I am making between me and you and every living creature with you, a covenant for all generations to come. I have set my rainbow in the clouds, and it will be the sign of the covenant between me and the earth. Whenever I bring clouds over the earth and the rainbow appears in the clouds, I will remember my covenant between me and you and all living creatures of every kind. Never again will the waters become a flood to destroy all life."

From Noah's three sons (Shem, Ham, and Japheth) came all the people who populate the earth today.

ABRAHAM, ISAAC, AND JACOB

Abram came out of the line of Shem, and he loved the Lord. The Lord told Abram, "Leave your native country, your relatives, and your father's family, and go to the land that I will show you." Abram obeyed.

Then God said to him, "This is my covenant with you: I will make you the father of not just one nation, but a multitude of nations! What's more, I am changing your name. It will no longer be Abram; now you will be known as Abraham, for you will be the father of many nations."

When Abraham was one hundred years old and his wife, Sarah, was ninety years old, they had a son and named him Isaac. A few years later God tested Abraham's faith. God asked Abraham to sacrifice Isaac as a burnt offering. As Abraham was obeying, the angel of the Lord stopped him. Because he did not withhold his son, Abraham was greatly blessed by the Lord.

Though Abraham had other children, God established his covenant with Isaac and his descendants.

Isaac had two sons, Esau and Jacob. Before Isaac died, he gave his blessing to Jacob.

One night when Jacob was alone, a man came up to him. This man and Jacob started wrestling with one another. They wrestled all night, and when the man saw that he could not overpower Jacob, he reached down and touched Jacob's hip and twisted it out of place. But Jacob still didn't let him go.

Then the man said to Jacob, "Let me go because it is almost daybreak."

Jacob replied, "I will not let you go unless you bless me."

The man asked him, "What is your name?"

"Jacob," he answered.

Then the man said, "Your name will no longer be Jacob but Israel *(the name God chose to be His nation)*, because you have struggled with God and with man and have overcome." (Israel is the Promised Land that God gives His people later.)

Jacob said, "Please tell me your name."

But the man said, "Why do you ask my name?" Then he gave Jacob his blessing.

So Jacob called that place Peniel (which means "face of God"), saying, "It is because I saw God face to face, yet my life has been spared."

Israel (Jacob) prospered because of God's blessing on him. His descendants greatly increased and became the Israelite people.

Sometime later the Israelites settled in Egypt. As the population of Hebrew people multiplied, the Egyptians became afraid that they would be overpowered by them. So the Egyptians enslaved the Hebrews to prevent them from becoming strong enough to overpower them. But the Lord blessed the Hebrew women in childbirth and they kept multiplying.

Pharaoh became worried because the Hebrew people kept growing in numbers, so he gave orders to throw all newborn Hebrew boys into the Nile River. There was great mourning in Egypt during this time.

MOSES

Exodus 2-11

A man of the house of Levi married a Levite woman. She became pregnant and gave birth to a son. When she saw that he was a fine child, she feared for his life since Pharoah ordered all newborn Hebrew boys to be thrown into the Nile River. So she hid him for three months. But when she could hide him no longer, she got a papyrus basket for him and coated it with tar and pitch. Then she placed the child in it and put it among the reeds along the bank of the Nile.

Pharaoh's daughter went down to the Nile to bathe. She saw the basket among the reeds and sent her slave girl to get it. She opened it and saw the baby. He was crying and she felt sorry for him. "This is one of the Hebrew babies," she said. She decided to keep the baby and raise him as her son. She named him Moses, saying, "I drew him out of the water."

The Hebrews were slaves in Egypt. After Moses had grown up, he went out to where his own people were and watched them at their hard labor. One day he saw an Egyptian beating a Hebrew. He looked around and, seeing no one, killed the Egyptian and hid him in the sand.

When Pharaoh heard of this he tried to kill Moses, but Moses fled from Pharaoh and went to live in Midian.

The Israelites had been in slavery for four hundred years, and God heard their cries for help. He decided it was time to set His people free from the Egyptians.

Moses was tending the flock of Jethro, his father-in-law and the priest of Midian, when he led the flock to the far side of the desert and came to Horeb, the mountain of God. There the angel of the Lord appeared to him in flames of fire from within a bush. Moses saw that though the bush was on fire, it did not burn up. So Moses thought, "I will go over and see this strange sight—why the bush does not burn up."

When the Lord saw that he had gone over to look, God called to him from within the bush, "Moses! Moses!"

And Moses said, "Here I am."

"Do not come any closer," God said. "Take off your sandals, for the place where you are standing is holy ground." Then He said, "I am the God of your father— the God of Abraham, the God of Isaac, and the God of Jacob."

At this, Moses hid his face because he was afraid to look at God. The Lord said, "I have indeed seen the misery of my people in Egypt. I have heard them crying out because of their slave drivers, and I am concerned about their suffering. So I have come down to rescue them from the hand of the Egyptians and to bring them up out of that land into a good and spacious land, a land flowing with milk and honey. And now the cry of the Israelites has reached me, and I have seen the way the Egyptians are oppressing them. So now, go. I am sending you to Pharaoh to bring my people the Israelites out of Egypt."

Moses agreed to go back and lead his people out of Egypt, and God was with him. Moses and Aaron (Moses' brother) brought together all the elders of the Israelites. Aaron told them everything the Lord had said to Moses. He also performed signs before the people, and they believed. When they heard that the Lord was concerned about them and had seen their misery, they bowed down and worshiped Him.

Afterward Moses and Aaron went to Pharaoh and said, "This is what the Lord, the God of Israel, says: 'Let my people go, so that they may hold a festival to me in the desert.'"

Pharaoh said, "Who is the Lord that I should obey him and let Israel go? I do not know the Lord and I will not let Israel go."

Moses and Aaron were persistent with Pharaoh about letting the Israelites go, but he refused to let them go. Then the Lord said to Moses, "Now you will see what I will do to Pharaoh: Because of my mighty hand he will let them go; because of my mighty hand he will drive them out of his country."

So the Lord said, "I will send plagues on the Egyptians and their animals until Pharaoh lets my people go."

These were the plagues that God sent to Egypt. It wasn't until the last plague—the death of their first-born—that Pharaoh finally agreed to free the Hebrews from slavery:

1. The Plague of Blood

2. The Plague of Frogs

3. The Plague of Gnats

4. The Plague of Flies

5. The Plague on Livestock

6. The Plague of Boils

7. The Plague of Hail

8. The Plague of Locusts

9. The Plague of Darkness

10. The Plague on the Firstborn

ISRAELITES SAVED BY THE BLOOD

The Tenth Plague – The Death of Egypt's Firstborn

Exodus 12–14

God told Moses to tell the people to kill a lamb or a goat (a year-old male without defect) and prepare it for a meal. They were to take some of the blood and put it on the doorframes of the houses where they ate this meal.

"On that same night," God said, "I will pass through Egypt and strike down every firstborn—both men and animals—and I will bring judgment on all the gods of Egypt. I am the Lord. The blood will be a sign for you on the houses where you are; and when I see the blood, I will pass over you—no destructive plague will touch you when I strike Egypt." The Israelites used the blood to mark their houses so their firstborn children would be spared.

The Israelites did just what the Lord commanded Moses and Aaron. At midnight the Lord struck down all the firstborn in Egypt, from the firstborn of Pharaoh who sat on the throne to the firstborn of the prisoner in the dungeon, and the firstborn of all the livestock as well. Pharaoh and his officials and all the Egyptians got up during the night, and loud wailing could be heard throughout Egypt, for there was not a house without someone dead.

During the night Pharaoh summoned Moses and Aaron and said, "Up! Leave my people, you and the Israelites! Go, worship the Lord as you have requested. Take your flocks and herds, as you have said, and go. And also bless me." The Egyptians urged the people to hurry and leave the country, "for otherwise we will all die!" So the people took their dough before the yeast was added and carried it on their shoulders in kneading troughs wrapped in clothing. The Israelites did as Moses instructed and asked the Egyptians for articles of silver and gold and clothing. The Lord gave His people favor with the Egyptians, and they gave them what they asked for.

When Pharaoh was told that the people had fled, he and his officials changed their minds about them and said, "What have we done? We have let the Israelites go and have lost their services!" So he had his chariot made ready and took his army with him—six hundred of the best chariots, along with all the other chariots of Egypt, with officers over all of them. The Lord hardened Pharaoh's heart so that he pursued the Israelites, who were marching out boldly. The Egyptians—all Pharaoh's horses and chariots, horsemen and troops—pursued the Israelites and overtook them as they camped by the Red Sea.

As Pharaoh approached, the Israelites looked up and saw the Egyptians marching after them. Terrified, they cried out to the Lord and said to Moses, "Was it because there were no graves in Egypt that you brought us to the desert to die? What have you done to us by bringing us out of Egypt? Didn't we say to you in Egypt, 'Leave us alone; let us serve the Egyptians'? It would have been better for us to serve the Egyptians than to die in the desert!"

Moses answered the people, "Do not be afraid. Stand firm and you will see the deliverance the Lord will bring you today. The Egyptians you see today you will never see again. The Lord will fight for you; you need only to be still."

Then the Lord said to Moses, "Why are you crying out to me? Tell the Israelites to move on. Raise your staff and stretch out your hand over the sea to divide the water so that the Israelites can go through the sea on dry ground. I will harden the hearts of the Egyptians so that they will go in after them. And I will gain glory through Pharaoh and all his army through his chariots and his horsemen. The Egyptians will know that I am the Lord when I gain glory through Pharaoh, his chariots, and his horsemen."

Then the angel of God, who had been traveling in front of Israel's army, withdrew and went behind them. The pillar of cloud also moved from in front and stood behind them, coming between the armies of Egypt and Israel. Throughout the night the cloud brought darkness to the one side and light to the other side; so neither went near the other all night long. Then Moses stretched out his hand over the sea, and all that night the Lord drove the sea back with a strong east wind and turned it into dry land. The waters were divided, and the Israelites went through the sea on dry ground, with a wall of water on their right and on their left. The Egyptians pursued them, and all Pharaoh's horses and chariots and horsemen followed them into the sea.

During the last watch of the night the Lord looked down from the pillar of fire and cloud at the Egyptian army and threw it into confusion. He made the wheels of their chariots come off so that they had difficulty driving. And the Egyptians said, "Let's get away from the Israelites! The Lord is fighting for them against Egypt."

Then the Lord said to Moses, "Stretch out your hand over the sea so that the waters may flow back over the Egyptians and their chariots and horsemen." Moses stretched out his hand over the sea, and at day-break the sea went back to its place. The Egyptians were fleeing toward it, and the Lord swept them into the sea. The water flowed back and covered the chariots and horsemen—the entire army of Pharaoh. Not one of them survived. But the Israelites went through the sea on dry ground, with a wall of water on their right and on their left. That day the Lord saved Israel from the hands of the Egyptians, and Israel saw the Egyptians lying dead on the shore. And when the Israelites saw the great power the Lord displayed against the Egyptians, the people feared the Lord and put their trust in Him and in Moses His servant.

GOD GIVES THEM THE LAW

Exodus 20 – Joshua 1

As Moses was leading the Israelites through the desert, God called Moses to come up on the mountain where He gave Moses these instructions for the people, called the Ten Commandments.

1. "I am the Lord your God, who rescued you from slavery in Egypt. Do not worship any other gods besides me.

2. "Do not make idols of any kind, whether in the shape of birds or animals or fish. You must never worship or bow down to them, for I, the Lord your God, am a jealous God who will not share your affection with any other god! I do not leave unpunished the sins of those who hate me, but I punish the children for the sins of their parents to the third and fourth generations. But I lavish

my love on those who love me and obey my commands, even for a thousand generations.

3. "Do not misuse the name of the Lord your God. The Lord will not let you go unpunished if you misuse his name.

4. "Remember to observe the Sabbath day by keeping it holy. Six days a week are set apart for your daily duties and regular work, but the seventh day is a day of rest dedicated to the Lord your God. On that day no one in your household may do any kind of work. This includes you, your sons and daughters, your male and female servants, your livestock, and any foreigners living among you. For in six days the Lord made the heavens, the earth, the sea, and everything in them; then he rested on the seventh day. That is why the Lord blessed the Sabbath day and set it apart as holy.

5. "Honor your father and mother. Then you will live a long, full life in the land the Lord your God will give you.

6. "Do not murder.

7. "Do not commit adultery.

8. "Do not steal.

9. "Do not testify falsely against your neighbor.

10. "Do not covet your neighbor's house. Do not covet your neighbor's wife, male or female servant, ox or donkey, or anything else your neighbor owns."

God gave them these laws to show the people what they would have to do to be perfect for heaven. In His wisdom, He knew they would not be able to follow all of them in their sinful nature. But He wanted them to know it too. Romans 3:20 (NIV) states, "Therefore no one will be declared righteous in his sight by observing the law; rather, through the law we become conscious of sin." But the people did not realize what God's plan was. They thought they would be earning their way to heaven by following these laws as closely as possible. They just didn't understand that even one mistake would cause them to be impure and would keep them from entering heaven. Therefore, they didn't understand that they needed a *Savior*—someone to rescue them from being thrown into hell.

49

Moses led the people across the desert and into the land of Moab. He led them up to the Jordan River, and on the other side of the river was the Promised Land that the Lord told them about. They were close enough that Moses and the people could see it.

Moses was getting older and his health was failing him. Before Moses died, he called Joshua, son of Nun, who was full of the Spirit of wisdom, and laid his hands on him. So the people of Israel obeyed Joshua as he led them to the Promised Land just as the Lord had commanded Moses.

Joshua led the people into the land promised by God. The Lord was with them as they overtook this land, which became the nation of Israel.

DAVID FACES GOLIATH

1 Samuel 17

A man named Jesse had eight sons, the youngest being David. Jesse's three oldest sons had already joined Saul's army to fight the Philistines. Every now and then Jesse would send David to his brothers with some food, and he would report back to his father on how the battle was going. David was also taking care of his father's herd of sheep in Bethlehem.

Now the Philistines gathered their army at Socoh to come against the Israelites. Saul was the king of Israel at that time, and he countered by gathering his Israelite troops near the valley of Elah. So the Philistines and Israelites faced each other on opposite hills, with the valley between them.

A champion warrior named Goliath, who was from Gath, came out of the Philistine camp. He was over 9 feet tall. He had a bronze helmet on his head and wore a bronze coat of scale armor weighing 125 pounds; a bronze javelin was slung on his back. His spear shaft was like a weaver's rod, and its iron point weighed 15 pounds. His shield bearer went ahead of him. Goliath stood and shouted to the ranks of Israel, "Why do you come out and line up for battle? Am I not a Philistine, and are you not the servants of Saul? Choose a man and have him come down to me. If he is able to fight and kill me, we will become your slaves; but if I overcome him and kill him, you will become our slaves and serve us." Then the Philistine said, "This day I defy the ranks of Israel! Give me a man and let us fight each other." Upon hearing the Philistine's words, Saul and all the Israelites were dismayed and terrified.

For forty days, every morning and evening, Goliath would come out and mock the Israelite army. One day Jesse sent David with some food to his brothers, and while he was there Goliath came out from the Philistine camp. Then David heard him shout his usual taunt to the army of Israel.

David asked the men standing near him, "What will be done for the man who kills this Philistine and removes this disgrace from Israel? Who is this uncircumcised

Philistine that he should defy the armies of the living God?" What David said was overheard and reported to Saul, and Saul sent for him.

David said to Saul, "Let no one lose heart on account of this Philistine; your servant will go and fight him."

Saul replied, "You are not able to go out against this Philistine and fight him; you are only a boy, and he has been a fighting man from his youth."

But David said to Saul, "Your servant has been keeping his father's sheep. When a lion or a bear came and carried off a sheep from the flock, I went after it, struck it, and rescued the sheep from its mouth. When it turned on me, I seized it by its hair, struck it, and killed it. Your servant has killed both the lion and the bear; this uncircumcised Philistine will be like one of them, because he has defied the armies of the living God. The Lord who delivered me from the paw of the lion and the paw of the bear will deliver me from the hand of this Philistine."

Saul said to David, "Go, and the Lord be with you."

Then Saul dressed David in his own tunic. He put a coat of armor on him and a bronze helmet on his head. David fastened on his sword over the tunic and tried walking around. "I cannot go in these," he said to Saul, "because I am not used to them." So he took them off. Then he took his staff in his hand, chose five smooth stones from the stream, put them in the pouch of his shepherd's bag, and with his sling in his hand approached the Philistine.

Meanwhile, the Philistine, with his shield bearer in front of him, kept coming closer to David. He looked David over and saw that he was only a boy, ruddy and handsome, and he despised him. He said to David, "Am I a dog that you come at me with sticks?" And the Philistine cursed David by his gods. "Come here," he said, "and I'll give your flesh to the birds of the air and the beasts of the field!"

David said to the Philistine, "You come against me with sword and spear and javelin, but I come against you in the name of the Lord Almighty, the God of the armies of Israel, whom you have defied. This day the Lord will hand you over to me, and I'll strike you down and cut off your head. Today I will give the carcasses of the Philistine army to the birds of the air and the beasts of the earth, and the whole world will know that there is a God in Israel. All those gathered here will know that it is not by sword or spear that the Lord saves; for the battle is the Lord's, and he will give all of you into our hands."

As Goliath moved closer to attack him, David reached into his bag and pulled out a stone and put it in his sling. Then he started to run at him twirling his sling faster and faster. As he got closer to him, David released his sling and the stone flew out of it, traveling around 90 mph when it struck Goliath on his forehead. Goliath became dizzy, blacked out, and fell face down on the ground. David ran up to him and, before he came to, took Goliath's sword and cut off his head. When the Philistines saw that their hero was dead, they turned and ran.

DAVID BECOMES KING OVER ISRAEL

2 Samuel 5

All the tribes of Israel came to David at Hebron and said, "We are your own flesh and blood. In the past, while Saul was king over us, you were the one who led Israel on their military campaigns. And the Lord said to you, 'You will shepherd my people Israel, and you will become their ruler.'" When all the elders of Israel had come to King David at Hebron, David made an agreement with the elders before the Lord, and they anointed David king over Israel. David was thirty years old when he became king, and he reigned forty years. In Hebron he reigned over Judah seven years and six months, and in Jerusalem he reigned over all Israel and Judah thirty-three years.

David had a heart for God, and God said the Messiah (Savior) would come out of the line of David.

THE SCRIPTURES JESUS HAD TO FULFILL

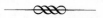

Now here is God's plan from the Scriptures step by step on how He was going to save us from our sins so we can be with Him and His Son in heaven.

Speaking through His prophets, God predicted these things would happen hundreds of years before they came to pass and through several different prophets.

Jesus came to do the will of His Father, which was to fulfill all these prophecies about His life, even the ones of His suffering and death so He could be the sacrifice for our sins.

Psalm 89:3-4 "The LORD said, 'I have made a covenant with David, my chosen servant. I have sworn this oath to him: "I will establish your descendants as kings forever; they will sit on your throne from now until eternity."'"

The Messiah was to come out of the line of King David.

Isaiah 7:14 "Look! The virgin will conceive a child! She will give birth to a son, and they will call him Immanuel, which means 'God is with us.'"

Mary was still a virgin when she conceived a child.

Micah 5:2 "But you, O Bethlehem Ephrathah, are only a small village among all the people of Judah. Yet a ruler of Israel will come from you, one whose origins are from the distant past."

Isaiah 9:6-7 "For a child is born to us, a son is given to us. The government will rest on his shoulders. And he will be called: Wonderful Counselor, Mighty God, Everlasting Father, Prince of Peace. His government and its peace will never end. He will rule with fairness and justice from the throne of his ancestor David for all eternity. The passionate commitment of the LORD of Heaven's Armies will make this happen!"

Caesar ordered a census to be taken so Joseph took Mary to Bethlehem to register because he belonged to the house and line of David. While they were there, Mary gave birth to a son.

Psalm 72:10 "The western kings of Tarshish and other distant lands will bring him tribute. The eastern kings of Sheba and Seba will bring him gifts."

The Magi traveled from distant lands to present Jesus with gifts of gold and incense and myrrh.

Jeremiah 31:15 "A cry was heard in Ramah—weeping and great mourning. Rachel weeps for her children, refusing to be comforted, for they are dead."

King Herod gave orders to kill all the boys in Bethlehem and its vicinity who were two years old and under.

Hosea 11:1 "I called my Son out of Egypt."

Joseph took Mary and the baby to Egypt to escape Herod; but after Herod died Joseph was told to return to Nazareth. And so it was fulfilled what was said through the Prophets: "He will be called a Nazarene."

Isaiah 40:3 "A voice of one calling in the desert prepare the way for the Lord; make straight paths for him."

John the Baptist was a messenger from God. He told everyone to ask for forgiveness for their sins, turn back to God, and be baptized. He baptized Jesus as an example for us today.

Isaiah 61:1 "The spirit of the Lord is upon me, for the Lord has anointed me to bring the good news to the poor. He has sent me to comfort the brokenhearted."

When Jesus was in the temple and handed the Scriptures to read, He opened up the scroll to Isaiah and read from it.

Isaiah 53:7 "He was oppressed and treated harshly, yet he never said a word. He was led as a lamb to the slaughter. And as a sheep is silent before the shearers, he did not open his mouth."

When Jesus was being questioned, He did not say a thing.

Isaiah 50:6 "I give my back to those who beat me and my cheeks to those who pull out my beard. I do not hide from shame, for they mock me and spit in my face."

They twisted together a crown of thorns and set it on His head. They put a staff in His right hand and knelt in front of Him and mocked Him. They spit on Him and took the staff and struck Him on the head again and again.

Isaiah 52:14 "Many were amazed when they saw him—beaten and bloodied, so disfigured one would scarcely know he was a person."

Jesus was so badly beaten you couldn't even recognize Him.

Matthew 20:18-19 "We are going to Jerusalem, where the Son of Man will be betrayed to the leading priests and the teachers of religious law. They will sentence him to die. Then they will hand him over to the Romans to be mocked, flogged with a whip, and crucified."

Jesus knew what was going to happen to Him, and He was telling His disciples what was about to happen.

Isaiah 53:5 "But he was pierced for our transgressions, he was crushed for our iniquities; the punishment that brought us peace was upon him, and by his wounds we are healed."

Jesus was going to the cross to pay for their sins, but they didn't realize what He was doing.

Psalm 22:16 "They have pierced my hands and feet."

They hammered nails through His hands and feet.

Psalm 22:18 "They divide my clothes among themselves and throw dice for my garments."

The soldiers cast dice for His garments.

Psalm 22:1 "My God, my God! Why have you forsaken me?"

About the ninth hour, Jesus cried out in a loud voice.

Psalm 69:21 "But instead, they give me poison for food; they offer me sour wine to satisfy my thirst."

One of them got a sponge and filled it with wine vinegar, put it on a stick, and offered it to Jesus to drink.

Psalm 34:20 "For the Lord protects them from harm– not one of their bones will be broken!"

They broke the legs of the other two; but when they came to Jesus, He was already dead so they didn't break His legs.

Zechariah 12:10 "They will look on me whom they have pierced."

They stuck a spear in His side.

Isaiah 53:9 "He had done no wrong, and he never deceived anyone. But he was buried like a criminal; he was put in a rich man's grave."

When the religious leaders questioned Him, they could not find Him guilty of any wrong.

Psalm 16:10 "...because you will not abandon me to the grave, nor will you let your Holy One see decay."

They found His tomb empty three days later.

Matthew 20:19 "...but on the third day he will be raised from the dead."

He was raised three days later.

THE BIRTH OF JESUS, THE MESSIAH

Luke 1-2

In the sixth month of Elizabeth's pregnancy, God sent the angel Gabriel to Nazareth, a village in Galilee, to a virgin named Mary. Gabriel appeared to her and said, "Greetings, favored woman! The Lord is with you!" Confused and disturbed, Mary tried to think what the angel could mean.

"Don't be afraid, Mary," the angel told her, "for you have found favor with God! You will conceive and give birth to a son, and you will name Him Jesus. He will be very great and will be called the Son of the Most High. The Lord God will give Him the throne of His ancestor David. And He will reign over Israel forever; His kingdom will never end!"

Mary asked the angel, "But how can this happen? I am a virgin."

The angel replied, "The Holy Spirit will come upon you, and the power of the Most High will overshadow you. So the baby to be born will be holy, and He will be called the Son of God. What's more, your relative Elizabeth has become pregnant in her old age! People used to say she was barren, but she's now in her sixth month. For nothing is impossible with God."

Mary responded, "I am the Lord's servant. May everything you have said about me come true." And then the angel left her.

Mary was engaged to be married to a man named Joseph, a descendant of King David. But before the marriage took place, while she was still a virgin, she became pregnant through the power of the Holy Spirit.

Joseph, her fiancé, was a good man and did not want to disgrace her publicly, so he decided to break the engagement quietly.

As he considered this, an angel of the Lord appeared to him in a dream. "Joseph, son of David," the angel said, "do not be afraid to take Mary as your wife. For the child within her was conceived by the Holy Spirit. And she will have a son, and you are to name Him Jesus, for He will save His people from their sins."

All of this occurred to fulfill the Lord's message through His prophet Isaiah (7:14), "Look! The virgin will conceive a child! She will give birth to a son, and they will call him Immanuel, which means 'God is with us.'" When Joseph woke up, he did as the angel of the Lord commanded and took Mary as his wife. But he did not have sexual relations with her until her son was born. And Joseph named Him Jesus.

At that time the Roman emperor, Augustus, decreed that a census should be taken throughout the Roman Empire. (This was the first census taken when Quirinius was governor of Syria.) All returned to their own ancestral towns to register for the census. And because Joseph was a descendant of King David, he had to go to Bethlehem in Judea, David's ancient home as predicted in Micah 5:2. He traveled there from the village of Nazareth in Galilee. He took with him Mary, his fiancée, who was now obviously pregnant. And while they were there, the time came for her baby to be born. She gave birth to her first child, a son. She wrapped Him snugly in strips of cloth and laid Him in a manger, because there was no lodging available for them (Isa. 9:6-7).

Jesus was born in Bethlehem in Judea, during the reign of King Herod. About that time some wise men from eastern lands arrived in Jerusalem, asking, "Where is the newborn king of the Jews? We saw His star as it rose, and we have come to worship Him." (Isa. 9:2: "We saw a great light.")

King Herod was deeply disturbed when he heard this, as was everyone in Jerusalem. He called a meeting of the leading priests and teachers of religious law and asked, "Where is the Messiah supposed to be born?"

"In Bethlehem in Judea," they said, "for this is what the prophet wrote: [Micah 5:2] 'And you, O Bethlehem in the land of Judah, are not least among the ruling cities of Judah, for a ruler will come from you who will be the shepherd for my people Israel.'"

Herod called for a private meeting with the wise men, and he learned from them the time when the star first appeared. Then he told them, "Go to Bethlehem and search carefully for the child. And when you find Him, come back and tell me so that I can go and worship Him too!"

After this meeting, the wise men went on their way. And the star they had seen in the east guided them to

Bethlehem. It went ahead of them and stopped over the place where the child was. When they came to the place where the star had stopped, they were filled with joy. They entered the house and saw the child with His mother, Mary, and they bowed down and worshiped Him. Then they opened their treasure chests and gave Him gifts of gold, frankincense, and myrrh as told in Psalm 72:10. When it was time to leave, they returned to their own country by another route, for God had warned them in a dream not to return to Herod.

THE ESCAPE TO EGYPT

Matthew 2:13-18

After the wise men had gone, an angel of the Lord appeared to Joseph in a dream. "Get up! Flee to Egypt with the child and his mother," the angel said. "Stay there until I tell you to return, because Herod is going to search for the child to kill him."

When Herod realized that the wise men had out-witted him. He became furious and sent soldiers to kill all the boys in and around Bethlehem who were two years old and under, based on the wise men's report of the star's first appearance. Herod's brutal action fulfilled what God had spoken through the prophet Jeremiah "A cry was heard in Ramah— weeping and great mourning. Rachel weeps for her children, refusing to be comforted, for they are dead." (Jer. 31:15)

So Joseph left for Egypt with the child and Mary, his mother, and they stayed there until Herod's death. This fulfilled what the Lord had spoken through the prophet: "I called my Son out of Egypt." (Hosea 11:1)

THE RETURN TO NAZARETH

Matthew 2:19-23

When Herod died, an angel of the Lord appeared in a dream to Joseph in Egypt. "Get up!" the angel said. "Take the child and His mother back to the land of Israel, because those who were trying to kill the child are dead." So Joseph got up and returned to the land of Israel with Jesus and His mother. But when he learned that the new ruler of Judea was Herod's son Archelaus, he was afraid to go there. Then, after being warned in a dream, he left for the region of Galilee. So the family went and lived in a town called Nazareth. This fulfilled what the prophets had said: "He will be called a Nazarene."

As Hosea 11:1 (NIV) said, "...out of Egypt I called my son."

JESUS PREDICTS HIS DEATH

John 8:28-30 (NIV) tells us, "So Jesus said, 'When you have lifted up the Son of Man, then you will know that I am [the one I <u>claim</u> to be] and that I do nothing on my own but speak just what the Father has taught me. The one who sent me is with me; he has not left me alone, for I always do what pleases him.' Even as he spoke, many put their faith in him."

Jesus replied, "The hour has come for the Son of Man to be glorified. I tell you the truth, unless a kernel of wheat falls to the ground and dies, it remains only a single seed. But if it dies, it produces many seeds. The man who loves his life will lose it, while the man who hates his life in this world will keep it for eternal life. Whoever serves me must follow me; and where I am, my servant also will be. My Father will honor the one who serves me" (John 12:23-26).

Now as Jesus was going up to Jerusalem, He took the twelve disciples aside and said to them, "We are going up to Jerusalem, and the Son of Man will be betrayed to the chief priests and the teachers of the law. They will condemn him to death and will turn him over to the Gentiles to be mocked and flogged and crucified. On the third day he will be raised to life!" (Matt. 20:18-19 NIV). This is in agreement with the Old Testament prediction that His body would not see decay (Ps. 16:10). He also told them,

"As you know, Passover begins in two days, and the Son of Man will be handed over to be crucified" (Matt. 26:2 NLT).

"One of you who has just eaten from this bowl with me will betray me. For the Son of Man must die, as the Scriptures declared long ago. But how terrible it will be for the one who betrays him. It would be far better for that man if he had never been born!" (Matt. 26:23-24 NLT).

"Each of you drink from it, for this is my blood, which confirms the covenant between God and his people. It is poured out as a sacrifice to forgive the sins of many" (Matt.26: 27-28 NLT).

JESUS KNEW THE SUFFERING HE WAS ABOUT TO GO THROUGH

John 12:27-28 (NLT): "Now my soul is deeply troubled. Should I pray, 'Father, save me from this hour'? But this is the very reason I came! Father, bring glory to your name."

After they finished eating, Jesus led them out into the Garden of Gethsemane where He was going to be arrested. Before they came to arrest Him, Jesus told them to "sit here while I go over there and pray."

He took Peter and Zebedee's two sons, James and John, and He became anguished and distressed. He told them, "My soul is crushed with grief to the point of death. Stay here and keep watch with me." He prayed, "My Father, if it is at all possible, let this cup of suffering be taken away from me. Yet I want your will to be done, not mine."

Then He returned to the disciples and found them asleep. Jesus left them a second time and prayed, "My Father, if this cup cannot be taken away unless I drink it, your will be done."

He returned to them again and found them sleeping. So He went to pray a third time saying the same things again.

Jesus knew the kind of suffering He was about to go through, and He asked His Father three times if it was possible to take this cup of suffering from Him. He was asking His Father if there was some other way that mankind could be saved from their sins. Jesus wanted to obey His Father's will. Jesus said, "I want your will to be done, not mine." God sent His Son to be the sacrifice for our sins, and Jesus obeyed.

(There is no other way or God would have provided it for His Son. So the people who claim that there are other ways to be saved are badly mistaken and false teachers. There is only one way and that is by putting your faith in God's Son, Jesus, who came and paid the ransom for our sins with His blood.)

Then He came to the disciples and said, "The time has come. The Son of Man is betrayed into the hands of sinners. Get up, let's go look. My betrayer is here!"

And even as Jesus said this Judas, one of the twelve disciples, arrived with a crowd of men armed with swords and clubs. They had been sent by the leading priests and elders of the people. The traitor, Judas, had given them a prearranged signal: "You will know which one to arrest when I greet Him with a kiss." So Judas came straight to Jesus. "Greetings, Rabbi!" he exclaimed, and gave Him a kiss.

Jesus said, "My friend, go ahead and do what you have come for." Then the others grabbed Jesus and arrested Him. But one of the men with Jesus pulled out his sword and struck the high priest's slave, slashing off his ear.

"Put your sword away," Jesus told him. "Those who use the sword will die by the sword. Do you not think I cannot call on my Father and at once put at my disposal more than twelve legions of angels? But how then would the Scriptures be fulfilled that say it must happen in this way?"

Jesus knew He could have asked His Father to save Him from the suffering He was about to go through. But He also knew He had to fulfill His Father's will so He could be the sacrifice for our sins. Jesus went through that suffering so that whoever puts their trust in Him will have their sins forgiven, and His Father will grant them entrance into His kingdom.

Inside, the leading priests and the entire high council tried to find witnesses who would lie about Jesus so they could put Him to death. But even though many agreed to give false witness, they could not use anyone's testimony. Finally, two men came forward who declared, "This man said, 'I am able to destroy the temple of God and rebuild it in three days.'"

The high priest stood up and said to Jesus, "Well, aren't you going to answer these charges? What do you have to say for yourself?"

But Jesus remained silent.

Then the high priest said to Him, "I demand in the name of the living God—tell us if you are the Messiah, the Son of God."

Jesus replied, "You have said it, and in the future you will see the Son of Man seated in the place of power at God's right hand and coming on the clouds of heaven."

The high priest tore his clothing to show his horror and said, "Blasphemy! Why do we need other witnesses? You have all heard His blasphemy. What is your verdict?"

"Guilty!" they shouted. "He deserves to die!" Then they began to spit in Jesus' face and beat Him with their fists. And some slapped Him, jeering, "Prophesy to us, you Messiah! Who hit you that time?"

Some of the governor's soldiers took Jesus into their headquarters and called out the entire regiment. They stripped Him and put a scarlet robe on Him. They wove thorn branches into a crown and put it on His head, and they placed a reed stick in His right hand as a scepter. Then they knelt before him in mockery and taunted, "Hail! King of the Jews!" And they spit on Him and grabbed the stick and struck Him on the head with it. When they were finally tired of mocking Him, they took off the robe and put His clothes on Him again. Then they led Him away to be crucified (cf. Isa. 50:6).

He was so badly beaten that He could not be recognized, as was predicted in Isaiah 52:14 (but many were

amazed when they saw Him). His face was so disfigured that one would scarcely know He was a man.

Jesus knew all the suffering He had to go through
so we could be freed from our sins, and He was willing
to do it. So why would you want to try to get into heaven
by some other way? God provided His Son to be the
sacrifice for your sins if you will accept it. God wouldn't
have put His Son through all that suffering if there was
any other way for us to get into heaven.

THE CRUCIFIXION

Matthew 27:32-51

Along the way they came across a man named Simon, who was from Cyrene, and the soldiers forced him to carry Jesus' cross. And they went out to a place called Golgotha (which means "Place of the Skull"). The soldiers gave Him wine mixed with bitter gall, but when He had tasted it, He refused to drink it. After they had nailed Him to the cross, the soldiers gambled for His clothes by throwing dice. Then they sat around and kept guard as He hung there. A sign was fastened to the cross above Jesus' head announcing the charge against Him. It read: "This is Jesus, the King of the Jews."

Two revolutionaries were crucified with Him, one on His right and one on His left. The people passing by shouted abuse, shaking their heads in mockery. "Look at you now!" they yelled at Him. "You said you were going to destroy the temple and rebuild it in three days [cf. Matt. 20:19]. Well then, if you are the Son of God, save yourself and come down from the cross!"

The leading priests, the teachers of religious law, and the elders also mocked Jesus. "He saved others," they scoffed, "but He can't save Himself! So He is the King of Israel, is He? Let Him come down from the cross right now and we will believe in Him! He trusted God, so let God rescue Him now if He wants Him! For He said, 'I am the Son of God.'" Even the revolution-aries who were crucified with Him ridiculed Him in the same way.

At noon, darkness fell across the whole land. At about three o'clock, Jesus called out with a loud voice, "Eli, Eli, lema sabachthani?" which means, "My God, my God, why have you abandoned me?" (Ps. 22:1 NLT).

Jesus knew that His mission was now finished, and to fulfill Scripture He said, "I am thirsty."

Some of the bystanders misunderstood and thought He was calling for the prophet Elijah. One of them ran and filled a sponge with sour wine, put it on a hyssop branch, and held it up to His lips. But the rest said, "Wait! Let's see whether Elijah comes to save Him."

When Jesus had tasted it, He said, "It is finished!" Then He bowed His head and released His spirit (John 19:30).

At that moment an earthquake shook the ground and the curtain in the sanctuary of the temple was torn in two, from top to bottom.

It was the day of preparation, and the Jewish leaders didn't want the bodies hanging there the next day, which was the Sabbath (and a very special Sabbath, because it was the Passover). So they asked Pilate to hasten their deaths by ordering that their legs be broken. Then their bodies could be taken down.

ABOUT BROKEN BONES

Psalm 34:20 "He protects all his bones, not one of them will be broken."

Zechariah 12:10 "They would look on the one they had pierced."

The Romans were very inventive in coming up with different ways to make their prisoners suffer before they died. At this time they were hanging them from a cross; they would nail their hands and tie their arms up. Then they would bend their legs, mount a block of wood to the cross, and nail their feet to it. With a body hanging down from a cross like that, it would put pressure on the lungs and make it very hard for someone to breathe. So with the legs bent, they could push themselves up far enough to get a breath of air, but it would be very painful. And then it would also take longer for the person to die, which is exactly what the soldiers wanted.

Because the Jewish leaders did not want the bodies left on the crosses during the Sabbath, they asked Pilate to order that the legs be broken and the bodies taken down. With their legs broken they would not be able to lift themselves up to breathe, so they would die more quickly.

These Jewish leaders also knew what the Scriptures said of the Messiah in Psalms: "He will protect all his bones, not one of them will be broken." So they thought they would prove to the people that Jesus was not the Messiah He claimed to be because of His bones being broken. The soldiers, therefore, came and broke the legs of the first man who had been crucified with Jesus, and then those of the other. But when they came to Jesus and found that He was already dead, they did not break His legs. Instead, one of the soldiers pierced Jesus' side with a spear, bringing a sudden flow of blood and water.

These things happened in fulfillment of the Scriptures that say, "Not one of [his bones] will be broken"

(Ps. 34:20 NIV) and "They will look on me, the one they have pierced" (Zech. 12:10 NIV).

The apostle John "who saw it has given testimony, and his testimony is true. He knows that he tells the truth, and he testifies so that you also may believe" (John 19:35 NIV).

How upset the Jewish leaders must have been when their plan to prove that Jesus was not the Messiah He claimed to be had failed again.

As we are told in Isaiah, His body was so badly flogged and beaten that even His family and closest friends could not recognize Him (Isa. 52:14, written around 681 BC: "Just as there were many who were appalled at him—his appearance was so disfigured beyond that of any man and his form marred beyond human likeness.")

GOD'S PLAN IS COMPLETED

Before Jesus breathed His last breath He said, "It is finished." He was referring to the sacrifices for sins; He was the final sacrifice for sins. There was no more need for animal sacrifices because He took the place of the lamb so that sin would be forgiven once and for all.

When Jesus died, the curtain in the temple was torn in two from top to bottom. This curtain separated the Holy Place from the Most Holy Place where the high priest would go once a year to offer sacrifices for the sins of the people. God the Father split the curtain in two because it was no longer needed. Remember back when the Israelites made the curtain and how thick it was? No man could tear that curtain in two; besides, why would they—it had to be a God thing.

The sacrifice for sins was completed by His Son, Jesus, when He went to the cross. Jesus fulfilled all the Scriptures and His Father's wishes by going to the cross for our sins, which the Father had planned from the very beginning.

So now the old system of animal sacrifices is not needed anymore. That is why the Father split the curtain in two. The new covenant was just beginning and the old covenant had come to an end. There was no more need for animal sacrifices for sin. The Father provided a way for us to be saved by believing in His Son, and not by animal sacrifices. So you have to choose either to believe Jesus came to do the will of His Father, which was to go to the cross for our sins, or not believe in Jesus and die in your sins, which will lead to your death (hell) (Heb. 10:8-10).

THE BURIAL OF JESUS

Isaiah 53:9 "He had done no wrong and had never deceived anyone. But he was buried like a criminal; he was put in a rich man's grave."

As evening approached Joseph, a rich man from Arimathea who had become a follower of Jesus, went to Pilate and asked for Jesus' body. Pilate issued an order to release it to him. Joseph took the body and wrapped it in a long sheet of clean linen cloth. He placed it in his own new tomb which had been carved out of the rock. Then he rolled a great stone across the entrance and left. Both Mary Magdalene and the other Mary were sitting across from the tomb watching.

The next day, on the Sabbath, the leading priests and Pharisees went to see Pilate. They told him, "Sir, we remember what that deceiver once said while He was still alive: 'After three days I will rise from the dead.'

So we request that you seal the tomb until the third day. This will prevent His disciples from coming and stealing His body and then telling everyone He was raised from the dead! If that happens, we'll be worse off than we were at first."

Pilate replied, "Take guards and secure it the best you can." So they sealed the tomb and posted guards to protect it. Now the Roman soldiers would not let anything happen to the body in the tomb. If someone took the body from the tomb, the soldiers would be held responsible and put to death themselves.

PROPHECIES
OF HIS RESURRECTION

The Scriptures tell us in Psalm 16:10 (NIV), "you will not abandon me to the grave, nor will you let your Holy One see decay."

Jesus also tells His disciples in Matthew 16:21 (NIV) "that he must go to Jerusalem and suffer many things at the hands of the elders, chief priests and teachers of the law, and that he must be killed and on the third day be raised to life."

In Matthew 20:19 (NIV) Jesus informs them that He will be turned over to the Gentiles "to be mocked and flogged and crucified. On the third day he will be raised to life!"

And Luke 24:7 (NIV) states, "The Son of Man must be delivered into the hands of sinful men, be crucified and on the third day be raised again."

THE RESURRECTION

Matthew 28:1-10

Early on Sunday morning, as the new day was dawning, Mary Magdalene and the other Mary went out to visit the tomb. Suddenly there was a great earthquake for an angel of the Lord came down from heaven, rolled aside the stone, and sat on it. His face shone like lightning, and his clothing was as white as snow. The guards shook with fear when they saw him, and they fell into a dead faint. The angel said to the women, "Don't be afraid! I know you are looking for Jesus, who was crucified. He isn't here! He is risen from the dead, just as He said would happen. Come; see where His body was lying. And now, go quickly and tell His disciples that He has risen from the dead, and He is going ahead of you to Galilee. You will see Him there. Remember what I have told you."

The women ran quickly from the tomb. They were very frightened but also filled with great joy, and they rushed to give the disciples the angel's message. And as they went, Jesus met them and greeted them. They ran to Him, grasped His feet, and worshiped Him.

Jesus said to them, "Don't be afraid! Go tell my brothers to leave for Galilee, and they will see me there."

EYEWITNESSES
OF HIS RESURRECTION

*He appeared to several different people
over a period of forty days*

Luke 24

A fter He had risen from the grave, He met two of His followers walking to the village of Emmaus, which was seven miles from Jerusalem. As they walked along, they were talking about everything that had happened. As they talked and discussed these things, Jesus suddenly came and began walking with them. But God kept them from recognizing Him. They told Him some women from the group of His followers were at Jesus' tomb early that morning, and they came back with an amazing report. They said His body was missing, and they had seen angels who told them Jesus was alive. "Some of our men ran out to see, and sure enough His body was gone, just as the women said," they told Him.

Then Jesus said to them, "You foolish people! You find it so hard to believe all that the prophets wrote in the Scriptures. Wasn't it clearly predicted that the Messiah would have to suffer all these things before entering His glory?" Then Jesus took them through the writings of Moses and all the prophets, explaining from the Scriptures the things concerning Him. Then their eyes were opened and they recognized Him..

Then the two from Emmaus told their story to the disciples, how Jesus appeared to them as they were walking along the road, and how they had recognized Him. And just as they were telling about it, Jesus Himself suddenly stood there among them. "Peace be with you," He said. But the whole group was startled and frightened, thinking they were seeing a ghost.

"Why are you frightened? Why are your hearts filled with doubt? Look at my hands and my feet. You can see that it's really me. Touch me and make sure I am not a ghost, because ghosts don't have bodies, as you see that I do." As He spoke, He showed them His hands and feet. Still they stood there in disbelief, filled with joy and wonder.

Then He asked them, "Do you have anything here to eat?" They gave Him a piece of broiled fish and He ate it as they watched. Then He said, "When I was with you before, I told you that everything written about me in the law of Moses and the prophets and in the Psalms must be fulfilled." Then He opened their minds to understand the Scriptures. And He said, "Yes, it was written long ago that the Messiah would suffer and die and rise from the dead on the third day. It was also written that this message would be proclaimed in the authority of His name to all nations, beginning in Jerusalem. There is forgiveness of sins for all who repent. You are witnesses of all these things. Now I will send the Holy Spirit, just as my Father promised. But stay here in the city until the Holy Spirit comes and fills you with power from heaven" (Luke 24:44-49 NLT).

One of the disciples, Thomas (nicknamed the Twin), was not with the others when Jesus came. They told him, "We have seen the Lord!"

But he replied, "I won't believe it unless I see the nail wounds in His hands, put my fingers into them, and place my hand into the wound in His side."

Eight days later the disciples were together again, and this time Thomas was with them. The doors were locked; but suddenly, as before, Jesus was standing among them, saying, "Peace be with you." Then He said to Thomas, "Put your finger here, and look at my hands. Put your hand into the wound in my side [cf. Psalm 22: 16]. Don't be faithless any longer but believe."

"My Lord and my God!" Thomas exclaimed.

Then Jesus told him, "You believe because you have seen me. Blessed are those who believe without seeing me" (John 20:24-29 NLT).

THE EYEWITNESS TESTIMONY OF PAUL
(A DISCIPLE OF JESUS)

1 Corinthians 15:3-9: "I passed on to you what was most important and what had also been passed on to me. Christ died for our sins, just as the Scriptures said.

He was buried, and he was raised from the dead on the third day, just as the Scriptures said. He was seen by Peter and then by the Twelve. After that, he was seen by more than 500 of his followers at one time, most of whom are still alive, though some have died. Then he was seen by James and later by all the apostles. Last of all, I saw him, too, long after the others, as though I had been born at the wrong time. For I am the least of all the apostles, and, in fact I am not worthy to be called an apostle after the way I persecuted God's church."

JESUS RETURNS TO HEAVEN

John 16:28 (NLT) "Yes, I came from the Father into the world, and now I will leave the world and return to the Father."

The eleven disciples left for Galilee, going to the mountain where Jesus had told them to go. When they saw Him, they worshiped Him. And Jesus told His disciples, "I have been given all authority in heaven and earth. Therefore, go and make disciples [followers or believers of Jesus] of all the nations, baptizing them in the name of the Father and the Son and the Holy Spirit. Teach these new disciples to obey all the commands I have given you" (Matt. 28:18-20 NLT).

Then Jesus lifted His hands to heaven and blessed them. While He was blessing them, He left them and was taken up to heaven. So they worshiped Him and then returned to Jerusalem filled with great joy (Luke 24:50-52).

JESUS CAME
TO DO THE WILL OF HIS FATHER

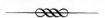

Isaiah 53:7-12 (NLT) "He was oppressed and treated harshly, yet he never said a word. He was led like a lamb to the slaughter. And as a sheep is silent before the shearers, he did not open his mouth. Unjustly condemned, he was led away. No one cared that he died without descendants, that his life was cut short in midstream. But he was struck down for the rebellion of my people. He had done no wrong and had never deceived anyone. But he was buried like a criminal; he was put in a rich man's grave.

"But it was the Lord's good plan to crush him and cause him grief. Yet when his life is made an offering for sin, he will have many descendants. He will enjoy a long life, and the Lord's good plan will prosper in his hands. When he sees all that is accomplished by his anguish, he will be satisfied. And because of his experience, my righteous servant will make it possible for many to be counted righteous, for he will bear all their sins. I will give him the honors of a victorious soldier, because he exposed himself to death. He was counted among the rebels. He bore the sins of many and interceded for rebels."

John 8:28-29 (NLT) "So Jesus said, 'When you have lifted up the Son of Man, then you will know that I am [the one I claim to be] and that I do nothing on my own but speak just what the Father has taught me. The one who sent me is with me; he has not left me alone, for I always do what pleases him.'"

Jesus said in John 6:40 (NLT), "For it is my Father's will that all who see his Son and believe in him should have eternal life. I will raise them up at the last day." (Just like He raised His Son back to life after He completed doing His Father's will.)

Hebrews 10:7 (NLT) "Jesus said, 'Look, I have come to do your will, O God – just as it is written about me in the Scriptures.'"

Hebrews 10:9-12 (NLT) "'Look, I have come to do your will.' He cancels the first covenant in order to establish the second. And what God wants is for us to be made holy by the sacrifice of the body of Jesus

Christ once for all time. Under the old covenant, the priest stands before the altar day after day, offering sacrifices that can never take away sins. But our High Priest [Jesus] offered himself to God as one sacrifice for sins, good for all time. Then he sat down at the place of highest honor at God's right hand."

LET'S REVIEW

We started out with God's plan for us. Before God created the world, He had a plan. His plan was to create people to be happy with Him in heaven—a perfect place. But He wanted us to choose Him as He chose us, so He gave us a free will.

In His foreknowledge He knew that we would not be able to remain perfect in order to enter heaven. And He planned for that too. When designing the world, He decided that there would only be one way to remove sin completely—and that was for someone to live a perfect life and shed his blood. He told us what we needed to know by sharing His thoughts and plan with us in the Bible.

The Bible tells us that God loved us so much that He sent His only Son to rescue us by enduring pain that was meant for us. He came down from His throne in heaven to be a sacrifice for the sins we committed.

So Jesus chose to come to earth and live the perfect life that His Father required, and to shed His blood on the cross to cover our sins. Our blood is impure because of the sins we commit under the law. Jesus kept all the laws so His blood was pure and acceptable to the Father for our sins.

Jesus accepted the plan and carried out His Father's will. With our free will, we can choose to trust His plan and obey the Father's will.

Let me give you something to think about: You should plan for your retirement here on earth, but how much more should you prepare for your eternal destination?

Here's an overview of what you've read so far:

- God started putting His plan into action. He created the earth.
- God created man to live on the earth. He gave Adam instructions on what he could and could not do. He gave Adam a free will to choose to obey His instructions or not to obey them. Adam chose not to obey God's command, and sin entered the world through his disobedience. We inherited this sinful nature.

- God set up a priesthood that would roll back mankind's sins until the time came when He would provide the proper sacrifice for sins once and for all. (His Son, Jesus, was that proper sacrifice for everybody's sins.)
- The Bible records the lives of different people who had a passion for God and were obedient to Him.
- God used blood to save the Israelite people's firstborn from being killed when He sent the death angel against the Egyptians.
- God gave us the Ten Commandments to live by, but what they actually did was show us why we needed a Savior.
- God told us the Messiah would come out of the line of David.
- Through His prophets, God told us His plan of how He was going to redeem us before it came to pass.

The Birth of the Messiah

A virgin would give birth, and He would come out of the line of David (Joseph was in the line of David).

He would be born in Bethlehem. Joseph, Mary, and the child Jesus escaped to Egypt because Herod was looking for the child so he could kill Him. After Herod died, they were called out of Egypt to return to Israel. They went to Nazareth and lived, fulfilling what the prophets had said: "He would be called a Nazarene." The religious leaders were looking for the Messiah to come out of Bethlehem, not Nazareth.

Jesus Started His Ministry

Jesus went to John the Baptist and was baptized. He started telling the people that He was the Messiah they had been waiting for. He was the one who would redeem them from their sins, and He came to do the will of His Father, which was to live the perfect life we couldn't so He could be the perfect sacrifice for our sins. His blood would be pure, which His Father required for the forgiveness of sins. Jesus didn't take credit for any of the miracles He performed but gave all the praise to His Father. Jesus told the people He was the way, the truth, and the life, and no one could come to the Father except through Him. There was no other way.

How He Was Going to Be Treated

Jesus would be handed over to the religious leaders, who would have Him flogged and then turned over to the Romans to be crucified. They would beat Him and do all kinds of humiliating things to Him before they nailed Him to a cross. He was so badly beaten that He was unrecognizable. Jesus knew this was going to happen to Him, and that is why He was in the Garden praying to His Father before they came and arrested Him. He pleaded with His Father three different times to "please take this cup of suffering away from me" if there was any other way, but He also said, "Not my will, but yours be done."

He knew it was for that hour He had come, but it still didn't make it any easier. He could have asked His Father to send Him a legion of angels to save Him from the suffering He was about to undergo, but He didn't. He was obedient to His Father and completed the work He came to do, which was to go to the cross and shed His blood for our sins. If there was some other way for us to be saved, God would have provided it. But instead Jesus was obedient to His Father's will and went through the humiliation and suffering on the cross for us.

Jesus on the Cross

Before Jesus breathed His last breath, He said, "It is finished," referring to the work His Father sent Him here to do. That work was to live the perfect life so His blood would be pure—untainted by sin—and then to shed His blood on a cross to cover our sins. He paid the penalty for our sins with His blood. We can stand righteous before God, but only if we accept His Son as our Savior. His blood covers everyone who will put their faith in His Son.

Other Beliefs

Jesus told us there would be many false teachers among us and that we need to be careful and not believe everything we hear. He told us to check out everything people teach against the Scriptures. There are not many ways to get into heaven as others teach. Jesus' Father would not have let His Son go through the death on a cross if there was another way. Jesus prayed to His Father and asked Him three times to take the cup of suffering away if at all possible.

His Body Would Not See Decay

Jesus told us that He would only be in the tomb for three days, and then on the third day He arose just as He said.

Eyewitnesses of His Resurrection

Jesus appeared to several different people over a period of forty days. He was seen by Peter and then by the Twelve. After that, He was seen by more than five hundred of His followers at one time.

Jesus Returns to Heaven

His disciples met Jesus on the mountain where He had told them to go. Then He told them to *go* and *make disciples* of all nations, *baptizing* them in the name of the Father and the Son and the Holy Spirit. He told them to teach these new disciples to obey all the commands "I have given you." Then He lifted His hands and ascended back up to heaven.

ABOUT THE APOSTLES
AND OTHER DISCIPLES

Peter and the other apostles were all put in jail for continuing to preach about Jesus. A Pharisee named Gamaliel (the teacher of Saul whose name was changed to Paul) was an expert in religious law and respected by all the people. He stood up and said to his colleagues, "Men of Israel, take care what you are planning to do to these men! Some time ago there was that fellow, Theudas, who pretended to be someone great. About 400 others joined him; but he was killed, and all his followers went their various ways. The whole movement came to nothing. After him, at the time of the census, there was Judas of Galilee. He got people to follow him; but he was killed, too, and all his followers were scattered. So my advice is, leave these men alone. Let them go. If they are planning and doing these things merely on their own, it will soon fail. But if it is from God, you will not be able to overthrow them. You may even find yourself fighting against God!" (Acts 5:34-39 NLT).

Jesus' apostles and some of His closest disciples were all killed for not denouncing that Jesus was who He claimed to be. This was some twenty to fifty years after Jesus' death. They were still proclaiming what Jesus had taught them. So if it was all a lie, they surely would not have died for a lie, not some twenty years later.

As Gamaliel said, "If it was of their own doing, it would have stopped a long time ago. But if it was from God, you would not be able to stop it, no matter how hard you try." Now it's been over two thousand years later, and God's Word is still being preached. So what they were teaching was from God. God will continue to protect His Word until He returns.

THE STORY ABOUT
THE SOWER AND THE SEED

Matthew 13

"Enter through the narrow gate. For wide is the gate and broad is the road that leads to destruction, and many enter through it. But small is the gate and narrow the road that leads to life; and only a few find it" (Matt. 7:13-14 NIV).

Jesus tells a parable about a farmer who went out and planted some seed, the seed being the Word of God. Some of the seed fell on the path. (The path is packed down dirt.) This represents those who hear the message about the kingdom and don't understand it. Their heart is hard and they don't believe in the Word. They think it is foolishness. Then the evil one comes and snatches away the seed that was planted in their hearts.

Some of the seed fell along the rocky places. These are the people who accept the Word and receive it with joy. But because they don't have deep roots, their faith only lasts a short time. When problems arise or they face persecution because of the Word, they quickly fall away.

Then there is the seed that fell among the thorns. These are the people who hear the Word, but the worries of this life and the deceitfulness of wealth choke it out making it unfruitful.

Lastly is the seed that fell on good soil. These are the people who hear the Word and truly understand it. They produce a crop of good fruit, yielding a hundred, sixty, or thirty times what was sown.

In the parable of the Sower and the Seed, three out of the four examples are people who are on the broad road (or the wrong path) that leads to destruction, and only one of them is on the narrow road (or the right path) that leads to eternal life. This means only 25 percent of the people are on the right path, and 75 percent of the people are on the path leading to destruction.

So most people are on the wrong path and don't even know it. They don't take the time to look into whether what they believe is really true or not. They are simply trusting in those who told them what to believe. This doesn't mean they're being led down the wrong path on purpose. Prior generations merely taught what they had been taught, with each generation doing the same thing. They were just passing it along without checking it out.

WE JUDGE BY HUMAN STANDARDS

Most people believe that they are good people. They judge themselves by human standards, and not by God's standard. You may ask, "What do you mean?"

Let me explain it this way:

If you would go up to someone on the street and ask them, "Do you consider yourself to be a good person?"

Most of them would say, "Yes, I believe I am a good person."

If you would ask them, "Would you go to heaven if you would die tonight?"

They would say, "Yes, I believe I would go to heaven."

I would then ask them, "Why do you think you would go to heaven?"

They might respond with something like this, "Well, I lived a good life," or, "I tried to do right by people," or, "I didn't kill anybody," or, "I think I would go to heaven."

So let's see how well we live our life according to God's standard--that is, the Ten Commandments.

"Have you ever told a lie?" If so, you are a liar.

"Have you ever stolen anything?" Even if what you've taken was as small as a pen or a paper clip from work, you are a thief.

The seventh commandment is Do Not Commit Adultery, but God said whoever looks at a woman or a man and lusts after them has committed adultery in his heart. "Have you ever looked at a woman or a man and lusted after them?"

Okay, so let's look at one more. The sixth commandment is Do Not Commit Murder. You may have said, "I haven't killed anybody." That's good. But God said, "Anyone who is angry with his brother will be subject to judgment." Did you ever get angry at someone?

Okay, by God's standard and because of His righteousness, you only have to break one of His laws to be guilty of being a law breaker.

Let me explain it this way:

Let's say you're hanging over a cliff and your holding on to a chain with ten links above you. If just one of those links were to break, you would fall to your death.

Now, according to human standards, you may look pretty good because you would say, "Well, everybody has done those kinds of things." And you would be right in saying that, because we all have.

But we are going to be judged according to God's standard, and we will be held accountable for every word we say. Matt. 12:36 "I tell you this, that you must give an account on judgment day of every idle word you speak." Rom. 3:23 "For all have sinned; all fall short of God's glorious standard." Now because of God's righteousness, we will have to be punished for the sins we committed in this life. (Rom. 3:20 "...For no one can ever be made right in God's sight by doing what His law commands. For the more we know God's law, the clearer it becomes that we aren't obeying it.")

God wants us to be with Him in His kingdom; but because of our human nature, He knew we could not live up to the standard that He required of us. So He sent His Son to live the life that He required, and then to be the sacrifice for our sins; so all who put their trust in His Son could be considered righteous when they stand before His Father, and then His Father will allow them to enter His kingdom for believing in His Son.

That is the kind of love the Father has for each one of us. So why would you want to try to get into heaven by some other way, or on your own good merits? If there was some other way you could have entered heaven, I assure you God would not have sent His Son down here to die on a cross for you. Take some time to think about that for a moment. Why would God send His Son down here to go through all that suffering for us, if we could have had done something ourselves to get us into heaven?

FORGIVENESS

Forgiveness is a word people use too casually. Many people believe they will go to heaven if they ask for forgiveness right before they die. They hear that God is all-forgiving and will forgive them if they ask. While this is true, there is more to it than that.

You can't ask for forgiveness without understanding what it means. It is one of those words that means nothing by itself. Just as "You're welcome" means nothing if said without "Thank you" being said first.

Forgiveness is a response. It is a response to being sorry for what you have done wrong. You can ask for forgiveness all day long, but if you are not truly sorry for the wrong you've done, the word means nothing. In order to be sorry and then forgiven, you have to know and admit your wrongdoing and then try your best not to repeat the mistake. Jesus said in John 8:11 (NIV) to a woman caught in adultery, "Then neither do I condemn you...Go now and leave your life of sin."

When you see your sin as God sees it (as an offense against Him) and are willing to turn away from that sin and ask for forgiveness, and you truly desire to follow Him, then He can use you.

This is where people fail to understand God's forgiveness. He does want to forgive and is ready to forgive all who ask. But He also knows if you are sincere and willing to try to change your ways. God doesn't want you to wait until the end of your life to live for Him. He wants you now. When you are sincere in wanting forgiveness and choose to follow Him, then He can use you for His glory.

Throughout the Bible the word used for being sorry is "repent." Over and over we are asked to repent and be baptized. God wants us to admit we are sinners, be truly sorry, and stop sinning. He also wants us to publicly profess Jesus Christ as our Lord. Being baptized is an outward demonstration of what you've done inwardly. He wants us to be proud of our partnership with Him and shine our light in this evil world so we can give hope to others.

Don't forget, Satan is in this world fighting for everyone to follow him to hell. He will use any means possible to trick you into thinking you're okay. He certainly won't be obvious in his maliciousness. 1 Peter 5:8 (NLT) says, "Be careful! Watch out for attacks from the Devil, your great enemy. He prowls around like a roaring lion, looking for some victim to devour."

While God doesn't need our help, He will use us for His glory if we allow Him to. He will be the ultimate winner of this battle and doesn't want any to go to hell—a real place of torment. (2 Pet. 3:9 NLT "...he is being patient for your sake. He does not want anyone to perish, so he is giving more time for everyone to repent.")

Why would God send anyone to hell? Because He is fair and just. When someone has been hurt and has gone to court, you always hear them saying, "I just want justice to be done." That brings us some peace.

Why is hell so horrible? Because God is not there. He is light and comfort. When He is missing, you have darkness and despair. Hell is a place of torment and fire. (Rev. 20:10 NLT "...was cast into the lake of fire... and they will be tormented day and night forever and ever.") But, remember, you don't have to go there. It is **your** choice.

GOD GETS THE GLORY

You may be thinking, "I believe that Jesus died for me and that we also must obey His commandments to be saved. As long as I'm good enough, I will be accepted into heaven."

But that is the thinking of earthly men. We judge ourselves by earthly standards. We do not think like God! If we have committed one sin, in God's eyes we cannot enter a perfect heaven. Besides, He either saved you when He died or He didn't. (There is no "He saved me, but..." or "He saved me, if...") Do you believe His death (by the shedding of His blood) alone saved you, or are you trying to earn salvation?

God wants us all to be with Him in heaven. That is why He prepared the way and asks us to trust His way. He created a plan that would be simple for us—*to accept* His gift of salvation (His death) with no strings attached. Yes, just accept His gift—that is, believe that

His blood has erased your sins. Believing and trusting, this is your free ticket to heaven. But we're the ones who make it hard. We can't believe God would make it that easy for us. But He did because He loves us! He told us, "For my yoke is easy and my burden is light" (Matt. 11:30 NIV).

God wants everyone in heaven to understand that His Son saved them from hell. It's not about what we have done but about what He has done for us. Jesus endured hell for us, when He did no wrong, to erase our mistakes.

Does that mean we can sin without worrying? No, because Hebrews 10:26 (NIV) says, "If we deliberately keep on sinning after we have received the knowledge of the truth, no sacrifice for sins is left. . . ." When we accept Jesus as the payment for our sins, He becomes our Master. We are asking for forgiveness. He now owns us and we have agreed to become His slave— a slave to righteousness which leads to holiness and eternal life in heaven.

Does that mean we will never sin again? No, we are asking for forgiveness and are promising to *try* not to sin anymore.

Paul said in Romans 7:18-19 (NLT), "I know nothing good lives in me, that is, in my sinful nature. I want to do what is right, but I can't. I want to do what is good, but I don't. I don't want to do what is wrong, but I do it anyway."

In our sinful nature we are constantly battling against doing what is right or what is wrong. We mess up sometimes, but that doesn't mean we lose our salvation. You see, it is not about how good we are. It's all about what Jesus did for us. Putting our trust in Him frees us from our sins. We ask our heavenly Father to forgive us of those sins and then we try to obey His commands. As long as we live on this earth we will keep on messing up from time to time, and God knows that. That is why God sent His Son to save us from our sins.

If you truly trust Jesus as your Savior, then you will try to obey His commands, which are to love the Lord your God with all your heart and to love your neighbor as yourself. As you grow in your relationship with God, you will start producing good fruit. These good fruits are not what save us, because we were saved by the blood of Jesus. The book of James tells us that faith without action is dead, meaning we show our love and obedience to God by our good deeds. The fruits of the Spirit are love, joy, peace, patience, kindness, goodness, faithfulness, gentleness, and self-control. Against such things, there is no law (Gal. 5:22).

WHO IS JESUS?

J esus Himself claims to be the Son of God! Now everybody agrees that Jesus actually lived here on this earth. But some have different thoughts on who He was. Some say He was a good teacher, others say He was a prophet, and still others call Him a liar.

When Jesus was standing before Pilate (the Roman governor) and being questioned, Pilate couldn't find any fault in His testimony. Pilate said, "I have examined him thoroughly on this point in your presence and find Him innocent." Then Pilate sent Jesus to Herod; he came to the same conclusion and sent Him back to Pilate.

When Jesus was being questioned by the religious leaders, they couldn't find any fault in Him either. Jesus came and lived the perfect life that His Father required of Him. His blood remained pure and unblemished and was used to cover the sins of many. His blood will cover the sins of everyone who accepts Jesus as their Lord and Savior. But God knows that not everyone will believe in what He did for them.

The only thing the religious leaders had against Jesus was when the high priest asked Him "Tell us if you are the Christ, the Son of God," and Jesus replied, "Yes, it is as you say." They claimed Jesus committed blasphemy. But if Jesus was telling the truth, it was not blasphemy. If Jesus had denied being the Son of God, He would not have had to go through the suffering of the cross. But Jesus said, "It was for this very reason I came" (John 12:27 NIV).

Jesus wasn't just a good teacher or a prophet. He definitely wasn't a liar. He would not lie even to keep Himself from being put to death.

Jesus claims to be the Son of God. And He told all the religious leaders that "in the future you will see the Son of Man sitting at the right hand of the Mighty One and coming on the clouds of heaven" (Matt. 26:64 NIV).

So if Jesus isn't a liar, and He tells us that He is the Son of God, and that He is the way, the truth, and the life and that no one can come to the Father except through Him, then there is no other way a person will enter the kingdom of God except by accepting Jesus Christ as their Savior (John 14:6).

After Jesus returned to His Father in heaven, the religious leaders had the apostles arrested. They wanted to put them to death for continuing to preach about Jesus even after they had been warned to stop. Peter told them they were going to obey God, not man. One of the Pharisees, whom they all respected, told the religious leaders, "Leave these men alone, because if it is from their own doing, it will fail; but if it is from God, you will not be able to stop it anyway." Here it is over two thousand years later and God's Word is still being preached. It has to be a God thing don't you think?

In Matthew 3:17, there was a voice from heaven that said, "This is my Son, whom I love; with Him I am well pleased." God, Himself, acknowledges Jesus as His Son.

OTHER BELIEFS

There are many different religions and cults in the world today and every one of them will tell you a different way of how to get into heaven. Jesus warns us about these false teachers who will lead you astray. They will be sincere in what they are teaching because that's what they have been taught. But Jesus tells us if their teachings do not match up with the Scriptures, they are false teachers. He calls them blind guides and says they, themselves, will fall into a pit. He said it was the blind leading the blind and that as your teacher falls into the pit, you too will fall into the same pit.

We are told in Acts 17:11 to be careful and to search the Scriptures to see if what others are telling us is true. Look at some of the false beliefs of others:

- There are many ways that lead to heaven and not just one.
- Jesus was a good man but not God's Son.

- Jesus will never come again.
- Jesus was not raised bodily from the grave.
- You just have to live a good life.
- Do more good things than bad.
- God won't send anybody to hell.
- Jesus was just a prophet.
- There is no heaven or hell.

Notice that some religions teach that we must earn our way to heaven. This leads people to think if they do more good things than bad things, they do not have to worry about where they'll end up.

But remember, we do not think like God. He will not let any sin into His perfect heaven. A person who only committed one sin would corrupt heaven. That is why we needed someone to cleanse us from sin. God knew it would be this way from the very beginning. When He created his plan, He provided a way for all of us to get to heaven even after we messed up. But He then asks us to believe and trust His plan. He will not allow anyone into heaven who thinks they were good enough for a perfect heaven. How arrogant they would be!! (Eph. 2:9 Salvation is not a reward for the good things we have done, so none of us can boast about it.) God wants everyone to be aware of the sacrifice His Son made to cleanse us. His SON did the work. That puts the rest of us on a level playing field—we are all sinners in need of a savior.

Jesus said in John 14:6 (NLT), "I am the way, the truth, and the life. No one can come to the Father except through me." So if He is the only way to the Father, there cannot be many ways that lead to heaven as some may think. Jesus also said in John 10:1 (NIV), "I tell you the truth, the man who does not enter the sheep pen by the gate, but climbs in by some other way, is a thief and a robber." In John 10:7-10 (NLT) Jesus said again, "...Yes, I am the gate. Those who come in through me will be saved... My purpose is to give them a rich and satisfying life."

Jesus clearly tells us that trusting in Him is the only way. Besides, if there were other ways to get into heaven, His Father surely would not have sent His Son down here to go through the humiliation and suffering that came with the death on a cross.

Jesus said, "For this is the very reason why I came."

Parents often raise their children in the religion in which their parents raised them. They really think that their way is the right way to get into heaven. They may never have read the Bible for themselves and are just taking the word of others whom they trust. I too was one of those parents and did not read the Bible until I was in my mid-forties. Then I started seeing some differences in what I was taught and what the Bible actually said about things.

Some churches teach that, when you are born, you inherit this original sin from Adam. They also say that if a baby would die, the baby would not be able to enter heaven because of this sin. So they started baptizing babies to remove this original sin.

While we do inherit a sin nature, we can't be accountable for our actions until we make the conscious choice to sin. This can't happen until we understand the difference between right and wrong. Babies begin as innocent humans. We learn how to act in this world to get what we want. It doesn't take long to learn that evil ways are often easier to do than the proper way. As children learn this, they eventually will need to make a choice—to follow God or to continue in sin. But until children can make their own spiritual decisions, they have nothing to be sorry for and, thus, no need to repent.

It is so important that you read the Bible. It is the only way to know if what you're being taught is correct. How horrible it would be to learn later in life that you taught your children wrong information about how to get to heaven! It would be very difficult to remedy this. If your children aren't taught to read the Bible at a young age, they will have a tough time understanding the importance of it when they are older. It will be hard for them to accept that their parents taught them false information. You don't want to be responsible for teaching your children or others false information that could lead to their spiritual death.

A STORY ABOUT HEAVEN AND HELL

In Luke 16:19-31 Jesus tells a story about a rich man and Lazarus. This is the only time Jesus uses a person's name in one of His parables.

There was this rich man who was well dressed and lived in luxury every day. Outside his gate lay a poor man named Lazarus who was covered with sores. As Lazarus lay there begging for scraps from the rich man's table, the dogs would come and lick his open sores. Sometime later, the poor man died and was carried by angels up to be with Abraham in heaven. The rich man also died and was buried, and his soul went to hell, also called the place of the dead. There, in great suffering, he saw Abraham in the far distance with Lazarus at his side.

The rich man shouted, "Father Abraham, have some pity on me! Send Lazarus over here to dip the tip of his finger in water and cool my tongue." Now that the rich man was in trouble, he wanted someone to have pity on him when he showed no pity to Lazarus when he was outside his gate begging for food. "Please, I am in great pain here in these flames," the rich man cried out.

But Abraham said to him, "Son, remember that during your lifetime you had everything you wanted, and Lazarus had nothing. So now he is up here in heaven being comforted, and you are in hell in great anguish. And besides, there is a great chasm separating us. No one can cross over to you from here, and no one can cross over to us from there."

Then the rich man said, "Please, Father Abraham, at least send him to my father's house. For I have five brothers, and I want him to warn them so they don't end up down here in this same place of torment."

But Abraham said, "They have the books of Moses and the prophets who warned them. Your brothers can read what they wrote."

The rich man replied, "No, Father Abraham! But if someone is sent to them from the dead, then they will repent of their sins and turn to God."

But Abraham said, "If they won't listen to Moses and the prophets, they won't listen even if someone

HOW GOD IS GOING TO DEAL WITH YOUR SINS

Their sins will remain on all who *have not* put their trust in what Jesus has done for them. On their day of judgment, they will stand before God and their book will be opened with all their deeds written down in it—the good and the bad. God will see the sins they have committed under the law, and the stain of that sin will still be on their heart—all because they did not believe in His Son. They tried to get in by their own way. Because of God's righteousness, He will not allow sin to enter heaven, so He will say to them, "Depart from me, you who are cursed, into the eternal fire prepared for the devil and his angels" (Matt. 25:41 NIV).

For all those who *did* put their trust in Jesus, their sins will be covered by His blood. On their day of judgment, they too will stand before God and their book will be opened with all their deeds written down in it—the good and the bad. God will not see the sins they committed because they will be covered by the blood of His Son, Jesus. They will be able to stand righteous before the Father—all because of the blood of Jesus. Then He will say to them, "Come, you who are blessed by my Father; take your inheritance, the kingdom prepared for you since the creation of the world" (Matt. 25:34 NIV).

THE BLOOD OF JESUS

God chose blood from the very beginning to be the factor on how He planned to save His people from their sins. This blood had to be pure and unblemished, and our blood was stained by the sins we committed under His laws. He sent His Son down here to fulfill what was said about Him in the Scriptures. His blood would be used to cover the sins of all those who put their trust in Him.

In the beginning of this book, we learned how God used blood to save His people from the death of their firstborn child. They were told to spread blood on the doorframes of their houses, and when the death angel came he would pass over the houses that had blood on their doorframes and spare their firstborn from death.

God used blood again to save us from His wrath because of the sins we committed while we were under the law. He sent His Son to fulfill what was written about

Him in the Scriptures—even the part where He would suffer and then shed His blood on the cross to redeem us from our sins. Our hearts are stained by the sins we committed, and the blood of Jesus washes away that stain. Jesus' blood is the only thing that can remove the stain that sin causes.

Look at it like this: You get a stain on your carpet and try all kinds of stain removals, but nothing works. The stain is still there. Well, that is like you trying to remove the stain on your heart by doing all kinds of good deeds. No matter what kind or how many good deeds you do, the stain will still be there. The only thing that will remove that stain is the blood of Jesus. Accepting Jesus as your Savior means that you trust in His blood to cover your sins.

At the Last Supper before Jesus was arrested, He took the cup and said, "Each of you drink from it, for this is my blood, which confirms the covenant between God and his people. It is poured out as a sacrifice to forgive the sins of many" (Matt. 26:27-28 NLT). Notice He said to forgive the sins of *many* and **not** to forgive the sins of *all*. Jesus knew that not everyone would

GOD'S GIFT TO YOU

Let's say you and your spouse liked to watch football just as my son, Bobby, and his wife, Hillary, do. And, let's say, you would like to go to the Super Bowl someday but you just cannot afford to buy the tickets plus the added expense of getting there. Suppose one of your friends came up to you and said, "Eric, my boss said he had two extra tickets to the Super Bowl and asked if anyone knew of two people who would like to go to the game." He went on to say that he had offered the tickets to Mike, Chris, Brian, and Jessica (who were his children). But none of them were able to go.

"I told him that I had two friends who would love to go."

So he gave me the two extra tickets and he told me that these tickets would cover the full expenses of the trip. He said that the tickets would cover the trip there and back plus the motel room and all the food while you were away--even at the ballpark. If you accept those tickets, you would have a free pass to get into the stadium, watch the game, and enjoy the whole experience of getting away without the worry of how much it was going to cost you, because the tickets covered the whole trip.

In the same way, if you would accept what Jesus did for you on the cross, you will have a free pass to enter heaven. Not because of anything you have done, but it is all about what Jesus did for you. That is the Amazing Grace that God gives in His Son.

But if you would have said, "Thanks, but I think we can get into the ballpark some other way without taking the tickets," you would just be fooling yourself. They will not let you in to see the game without having a ticket; and, if you don't accept Jesus as your Savior, you will not be able to enter heaven either. Just as you would be foolish to try to get into the ballpark without tickets when your friend gave you free tickets, you would be just as foolish to try to get into heaven by some other means because Jesus has already paid the price for you.

God sent His Son Jesus here to redeem us, to set us free from our sins because He knew we were unable to save ourselves. God knew we could not pay for the ticket ourselves, so He paid for the ticket for us with His Son's blood; and to all who accept His Son as their Savior, they will be accepted into His kingdom. All who believe in His Son will stand righteous before His Father in heaven. We can stand righteous before His Father, not because of anything we have done, but because of what Jesus has done for us. He paid our ticket in full. Remember, we all have sinned and fallen under God's wrath which will lead to our destruction. But God will show mercy to all those who accept His Son as their Savior and grant them Grace so that they can enter heaven. God said, "All who believes in my Son will be saved." There is only one way to get into heaven, and that is by believing in God's Son. All those who refused to accept His Son as their Savior will remain under God's wrath, and what a dreadful thing to fall under the wrath of the living God!

Now I don't want you to take my word for what I have written. I want you to check it out with what the Bible teaches. And if you find that it agrees with what the Bible teaches, then I ask you to accept Jesus as your Lord and Savior. I don't want you to try to get into heaven on your own works or by some other way.

I'm not saying to stop doing good deeds. I'm just saying not to trust in them to get you into heaven because your ticket has already been paid for by Jesus. Jesus tells us not to store up treasures here on earth but to store up your treasures in heaven where moth and rust won't destroy them. So keep on doing your good deeds as a way of saying thank you for saving me, and you will also be rewarded for all the good deeds you do here on earth when you get to heaven.

By accepting Jesus as your Lord and Savior, your name will be written in the Book of Life. Attending a bible teaching church will help you grow in your walk with the Lord. Heb. 10:25 ("Let us not give up meeting together, as some are in the habit of doing...)

BAPTISM

Before Jesus returned to His Father, He told His followers to go and make disciples of all nations baptizing them in the name of the Father and the Son and the Holy Spirit. (Matt. 28:19) Jesus, himself, was baptized to fulfill all righteousness and to also be an example for us.

There is one physical thing that God asks of us to do to prove our acceptance of Him, and it is not difficult. And that is to be baptized. It is a humbling experience letting someone lower you under water and raising you back up.

For me, this was a stumbling block for a long time. You see, I was baptized when I was a baby and I struggled with whether I was saved or not. I kept coming up with different reasons why I thought I was okay. I'd say I was confirmed when I was older, or in one part of the Bible it said the whole family was baptized; but it didn't mention any babies. You see I was trying to justify my salvation by doing it my way instead of God's way. That is why I searched the Bible so hard looking for somewhere in the Bible that told about a baby being baptized; and there just wasn't one. But I still kept putting it off. I don't know if it was my pride or an embarrassment or just plain stubbornness that kept me from being obedient and doing it God's way. Instead, I kept trying to justify it as being okay, but I never really had peace about it.

It wasn't until my daughter, Tracy, decided she wanted to be baptized that I decided to be obedient to God's Word and do it His way instead of trying to justify my way. Ever since then, I've had peace about my salvation.

Some people who were baptized when they were a baby have a hard time seeing the need to be baptized again. Some feel like they are being disrespectful to their parents if they get baptized again.

Well, here is another way to look at that. Let's say your parents owned a fruit stand and they charged their customers according to how much the fruit weighed. This went on for years and then they died and left the fruit stand to you. One day an inspector came in and checked your scales and found them to be off and you had been overcharging your customers. Now, you are using the same scales that your parents were using. So does that mean your parents were cheating their customers by overcharging them all those years? Of course not, because they did not know that the scales were off. But now that you know that the scales are wrong, you must adjust the scales so you won't be guilty of cheating your customers. So when you learn that something is not right, then you have a responsibility to correct it or you will be guilty of being in the wrong. Your parents would not be disappointed in you if you made a decision to get baptized again because you are trying to do the right thing, or trying to do it God's way.

Others may be embarrassed or are too stubborn to be baptized. Still others may feel it's too much trouble or don't want to take the time to do it.

Here is another thought: If you're going to raise a family, you are going to want to be sure that you're teaching your children God's way of doing things and not the way of others. When you get older, it is so hard to change what you believe--at least it was for me. But because God was patient with me and because I was searching for the truth, God opened my heart to His Word.

If you want to go before the church (or the Lord) and confess that you are going to raise your child up to know the Lord, there is nothing wrong with that. You need to raise your child up to fear the Lord. Proverbs 1:7 tells us that to "fear the Lord is the beginning of knowledge." Then we expand our knowledge by reading the Scriptures. God's Words tell us who will be saved and why. We should fear the Lord because He has the power to cast us into hell or have mercy on us and allow us into His kingdom.

Believing in what Jesus has done for you is your first step. The next step is proving you believe in Him by being obedient to His Word. James 2:19 says "You believe in one God. Good! Even the demons believe that--and shudder." And also in James 2:17, we read that "faith by itself, if it is not accompanied by action, is dead."

In Jesus' day, the Greek word for Baptize was Baptizo which means to be submerged or to dip under. I know a lot of people today have been baptized when they were infants. Being baptized is a personal decision that everyone needs to make for themselves and your parents cannot make that decision for you.

Babies weren't baptized until hundreds of years later when someone or some group of people decided that babies needed to be baptized in order for them to go to heaven. The Bible teaches us that we must repent of our sins and be baptized. Think about it, babies cannot repent of their sins. They haven't done anything wrong. They cannot do anything for themselves. They are totally dependent on their parents to take care of them. The people who changed the way to be baptized were trying to do it their way, and not God's way, when they started to baptize babies.

Some of the religious leaders (called the Sadducees) came up to Jesus and asked Him a question about people being married in heaven and Jesus replied, "You are in error because you do not know the Scriptures or the power of God." (Matt. 22:29) I believe the group of people who started baptizing babies was also in error because they didn't understand the Scriptures either; and they also didn't understand the power of God to protect the little children.

Jesus will protect the innocent children, and not until they mature and know the difference between right and wrong will they be held accountable for their own actions. They need to be able to understand the message of the cross before they are held accountable for their decision.

If those who made the decision to start baptizing babies are in error because they didn't understand the Bible (just like when Jesus told the religious leaders that they were in error because they didn't understand the Scriptures or the power of God), they would be false teachers or blind guides and those who follow that teaching are also blind. So, you see, you have to be able to believe in what Jesus has done for you. Then you need to be obedient to what He has told you to do. Jesus said in John 14:15, "If you love me, obey my commandments." And among His commands was to be baptized and to produce good fruit. Your parents cannot make your decision for you. You have to make that decision for yourself because you will be held accountable for your own actions.

STORIES ABOUT OBEDIENCE

The Bible contains many examples of people who were baptized immediately after accepting Jesus as their Savior:

The Day of Pentecost

On the day of Pentecost, after Peter and the other disciples received the Holy Spirit, Peter boldly got up in front of the crowd and explained to them that they had just received the Holy Spirit themselves. He began to explain to the crowd that Jesus, whom they had crucified, was their Lord and Savior.

The people that heard this asked Peter, "What shall we do?" Peter replied, "Repent and be baptized, every one of you, in the name of Jesus Christ for the forgiveness of your sins. And you will receive the gift of the Holy Spirit." Those who accepted his message were baptized, and about three thousand were added to their number that day. (Acts 2:14-41)

But not everyone accepted his message.

Philip and the Ethiopian Eunuch

The Spirit told Philip, "Go to that chariot and stay near it."

Then Philip ran up to the chariot and heard the man reading Isaiah the prophet. "Do you understand what you are reading?" Philip asked.

"How can I," he said, "unless someone explains it to me?" (Acts 8:29-31)

Philip began with that very passage of Scripture and told him the good news about Jesus. As they traveled along the road, they came to some water and the eunuch said, "Look, here is water. Why shouldn't I be baptized?" And he gave orders to stop the chariot. Then both Philip and the eunuch went down into the water and Philip baptized him. (Acts 8:35-38)

Saul / Paul

Saul, who later became Paul, was under the training of Gamaliel to be a Pharisee (a religious leader) and he was zealous for God. He was on his way to Damascus to persecute all those who were following this New Way [Jesus] when suddenly a bright light flashed around him and he heard a voice say to him, "Saul, Saul, why do you persecute me?"

"Who are you, Lord?" Saul asked.

"I am Jesus, whom you are persecuting," he replied. "Now get up and go into the city and you will be told what you must do."

Now Saul was blinded by this great light that flashed around him. So his companions led him into the city.

Now God appeared to Ananias, also, and told him to go to Saul and restore his sight. When Ananias arrived, he placed his hands on Saul and said, "Brother Saul, the Lord—Jesus, who appeared to you on the road as you were coming here—has sent me so that you may see again and be filled with the Holy Spirit." Immediately, something like scales fell from Saul's eyes, and he could see again. He got up and was baptized. (Acts 9: 1-18)

Cornelius

Cornelius and his family were devout and God fearing. He gave generously to the needy and prayed to God regularly. He was a good man and he did good deeds, but he still wasn't saved yet. (You see, being good doesn't save you.) While Peter was talking to them about Jesus, the Holy Spirit came upon them.

Then Peter said, "Can anyone keep these people from being baptized with water? They have received the Holy Spirit just as we have." So he ordered that they be baptized in the name of Jesus Christ. (Acts 10:47-48)

The Jailer

Paul and Silas were in prison at this time. There was a jailer in charge of the prisoners. Suddenly there was an earthquake and the prison doors were opened. The jailer was afraid that some of the prisoners had escaped.

You see, in those days if a prisoner escaped, the king would have the jailer who was in charge put to death. So the jailer started to kill himself with a sword;

but Paul shouted, "Don't harm yourself! We are all here!" So the jailer was thankful to Paul and Silas.

He then brought them out and asked, "Sirs, what must I do to be saved?"

They replied, "Believe in the Lord Jesus, and you will be saved—you and your household." (Acts 16:30-31)

Then Paul and Silas told them about Jesus. At that hour of the night the jailer took them and washed their wounds; then immediately he and all his family were baptized. (Acts 16:33)

Naaman

This is a story about a man named Naaman who was a good commander in the army, but he had leprosy. This is a skin disease that eats away the flesh and was not curable (2 Kings 5:2-16). He had taken captive a young girl from Israel, and she served Naaman's wife. She said to her mistress, "If only my master would see the prophet who is in Samaria! He would cure him of his leprosy." Naaman went to his master and told him what the girl from Israel had said.

"By all means, go," the king of Aram replied. "I will send a letter to the king of Israel." So Naaman left, taking with him ten talents of silver, six thousand shekels of gold, and ten sets of clothing. The letter that he took to the king of Israel read: "With this letter I am sending my servant Naaman to you so that you may cure him of his leprosy."

As soon as the king of Israel read the letter, he tore his robes and said, "Am I God? Can I kill and bring back to life? Why does this fellow send someone to me to be cured of his leprosy? See how he is trying to pick a quarrel with me!"

When Elisha, the man of God, heard that the king of Israel had torn his robes, he sent him this message: "Why have you torn your robes? Have the man come to me and he will know that there is a prophet in Israel." So Naaman went with his horses and chariots and stopped at the door of Elisha's house.

Elisha sent a messenger to say to him, "Go, wash yourself seven times in the Jordan, and your flesh will be restored and you will be cleansed."

But Naaman went away angry and said, "I thought that he would surely come out to me and stand and call on the name of the Lord his God, wave his hand over the spot and cure me of my leprosy. Are not Abana and

Pharpar, the rivers of Damascus, better than any of the waters of Israel? Couldn't I wash in them and be cleansed?" So he turned and went off in a rage.

Naaman's servants went to him and said, "My father, if the prophet had told you to do some great thing, would you not have done it? How much more, then, when he tells you, 'Wash and be cleansed'!"

So he went down and dipped himself in the Jordan seven times, as the man of God had told him, and his flesh was restored and became clean like that of a young boy. Then Naaman and all his attendants went back to the man of God. He stood before him and said, "Now I know that there is no God in all the world except in Israel."

God is very serious about being obedient. God sent His Son down here to fulfill all the prophecies written about Him in the Scriptures—even the ones about the suffering He would have to go through on His way to the cross. God didn't say, "Maybe you can skip that part" or "Maybe you can change it a little bit." No, Jesus fulfilled it completely, exactly the way it was written. So why should we think that we can change things to be done our way and not God's way?

If God's Son had to be obedient to His Father's will, then we should be obedient to His will also because once you have accepted His Son as your Savior, you become His adopted child. Why should He expect less from you than He did His Son? We should be grateful for what He did for us and want to do things God's way and not our own way. Besides, Jesus went through a lot of suffering to redeem you from your sins.

After Naaman was told what he needed to do to be healed, he became angry and went away in a rage because the prophet didn't do what Naaman thought he should do. Naaman wanted it to be done his way. His temper almost kept him from being healed. But because of his good friends, he was persuaded to go back and try what the prophet had told him to do. He obeyed and God cured him—not because the Jordan River was special or the water was cleaner, but because of his obedience to what Elisha had told him.

What if Naaman, when he got to the Jordan River, said, "Oh, this is too cold! I'm not going in there!" And what if he then stopped, cupped his hands, and just poured water over his head? Do you think God would have cured him?

When God told the people in Egypt to put blood around their doorframes to save their firstborn from being killed, what if they had said, "I'm not going to put blood around my doorframe. I'm just going to put some on my fencepost or on the door!" Do you think God would have honored that? Why would you want to take a chance by doing it your way instead of what God told you to do?

Naaman was told to go and dip himself seven times in the Jordan River to be cured. The people in Egypt were told to put blood around their doorframe to save their firstborn child. Abraham was told to sacrifice his son Isaac on an altar, and right before he did an angel stopped him. They were all blessed because of their obedience. We are told to be baptized (lowered under water and raised back up). That is the way they did it back in Jesus' day. We should obey.

When God tells us to do something, it is usually a simple task. But we think it can't be that easy and so we make it harder for ourselves because we don't truly understand the love of God. There is nothing hard about getting baptized. It is a simple and humbling act of obedience, but we make it harder than it is.

ANOTHER WAY
TO LOOK AT BAPTISM

Imagine that you and your partner want to get married. You plan your wedding and invite all your friends and family. When the day finally comes and the ceremony is ending, the minister pronounces you man and wife. You are ecstatic and you tell everyone that you are now married, and you make plans for your future together. You do this because, of course, you believe the minister when he says you're married.

But what if you did not believe him? You would not tell anyone you're married or plan a future together. You might think, "Surely there is something else I must do to be married—this is too simple!" While thinking like this, you would lose all the joy in marriage because you just couldn't believe you were married.

Likewise, Jesus has told you He came to save you from hell. He made the plans and did all the work necessary for you to be saved. But you have to believe Him. You can say it is too simple and keep doing the things you're doing. This is denying Him. No one can make you believe. We can only tell you it's true.

Nothing else needs to be done. When Jesus was on the cross, He said "It is finished!" He meant He had paid the penalty for sin once and for all, and you have been pronounced SAVED if you believe it. Then, if you believe you are saved, you act like it. You tell people you have been saved because you're proud of it, not ashamed. You now belong in Jesus' camp, not Satan's! You have been forgiven and are leaving your old way of life and starting on a journey with Jesus as your leader. And when you're proud of being saved, you want to be baptized to show the world you desire to do the Father's will just as Jesus did.

"Then Jesus came from Galilee to the Jordan to be baptized by John. But John tried to deter Him, saying, 'I need to be baptized by you, and do you come to me?' Jesus replied, 'Let it be so now; it is proper for us to do this to fulfill all righteousness.' Then John consented. As soon as Jesus was baptized, he went up out of the water. At that moment heaven was opened, and he saw the Spirit of God descending like a dove and lighting on him. And a voice from heaven said, 'This is my Son, whom I love; with him I am well pleased'" (Matt. 3:14-17 NIV).

God was pleased that His Son was baptized. Jesus said He did it to fulfill all righteousness. He was showing us what to do. If Jesus, the Son of God, can humble Himself to show us what to do when He was perfect, shouldn't we follow His way?

We have to let our pride go, humble ourselves, and follow Jesus. Jesus said we must become like little children to enter heaven. We certainly don't want to tell Him that being baptized into Him was too embarrassing or too much trouble.

A WORD ABOUT THE BIBLE

G od has protected His Word for over two thousand years, and He will continue to protect it until the end of time. God has given us the Bible so we will know what His will is for our life.

The Bible is our *instruction book* provided by God Himself. By inspiring its writers, God wanted us to know that though we can't get to heaven on our own, He provided what was needed for us to get there. The Bible was His way of sharing His thoughts with us, and it is written so that we may *know* we have eternal life (1 John 5:13).

When Jesus was walking with His apostles He told them stories in parables, but when He got to the end of His ministry He told them plainly what was going to happen.

God left us His Word, the Bible, and He didn't make it difficult for us to understand. Sometimes we try to find some hidden meaning or twist the words to say what our itching ears want to hear.

When you read the Bible, trust that Jesus will open your heart so He can reveal His Word to you clearly. Don't try to make it harder than it is. God is too smart to give us a Bible to live by that we couldn't understand. What purpose would it serve to give us His Word if we couldn't understand it? You don't need a college degree to understand the Bible. God has given His Word to everybody and not just to the learned.

There are many different versions of the Bible from which you can choose. Pick the one that speaks to you clearly and trust God to reveal His Word to you. As Jesus said, "Seek and you will find" (Matt. 7:7 NIV). Trust Jesus to keep His Word.

A WORD OF WARNING

L et's say you live out in the country but you work in
town. In order to get to work, you have to travel on
this narrow road that goes over a bridge to get across
a small canyon. You've lived in the country for years,
so you have traveled on this narrow road many, many
times.

Suppose one day you were on your way to work
and could barely see in front of you. It had stormed the
night before creating a heavy, dense fog. As it was a
country road, very few cars traveled on it, but on this
particular morning there was one car in front of you. So
you kept up enough speed to be able to follow its taillights. All of a sudden the taillights you were following
disappeared.

You started to wonder what could have happened.
You slowed down so you wouldn't run into the back of
that car. Then you noticed that the bridge was out so

you slammed on your brakes and came to a skidding stop right before going over the edge to your death, just as the car in front of you had done. You had a close call!

After you had calmed down, you realized that your son, Cory, travels that same road to work. You knew you had to warn him. You tried to call your son on your cell phone, but you couldn't get through. So you got back in your car, turned it around, and headed back toward his house hoping to catch him to warn him about what had happened.

As you rushed back down the road, you saw another car's headlights coming toward you. You rolled down your window and started waving your arm to get them to stop so you could warn them that the bridge was out. But it was so foggy they didn't see you. When the car passed you, you noticed that it was your son's car and he was driving. Now you started to panic. You stopped your car and tried to turn it around as fast as you could without getting stuck. Finally, you got the car turned around and then stomped on the gas to try to catch up with him before he got to the bridge.

As you got closer to him, you started blowing your horn, but he kept on going. Then you started flashing your lights on and off to get his attention, but that didn't work either. So you swerved into the other lane to pass him and then noticed that you were getting really close to the bridge. So you sped up, cut in front of him, and slammed on your brakes. He too slammed on his brakes to keep from hitting you.

He was furious. You got out of your car and started walking back toward him. Then he recognized it was you, and he wondered what the heck was going on. But when he got out of his car, he suddenly noticed that the bridge was gone. There was nothing there and he knew that he would have driven off the road and into the canyon to his death.

You both walked over to the edge of the road, looked down, and saw all the cars that had fallen into the canyon. Once he realized what you had done for him, he was grateful because he knew that you just saved his life.

That is what might happen when you tell your family and friends about the Good News of Jesus and what He has done for them. They may not want to hear it, but once they understand what He did for them, then they too will be thankful that you did not give up on them.

If they haven't accepted Jesus as their Savior, they will be like the ones driving off the road into the canyon to their death.

Jesus told us to share the Good News about Him with our friends so they can be saved also. Once you know the freedom and peace you have in Christ, you will want to tell others about Him, especially your family and friends, so they can also have this freedom and peace. You will tell them with the same urgency the man felt when driving the car to catch up with his son so he would not drive over the cliff to his death.

What if you and your friend are in a bad car wreck and you both are killed. You go to heaven and your friend doesn't make it because he/she hadn't heard about Jesus and what He has done for them. Then they look up and see you in heaven and cry out, "Why didn't you tell me about Jesus?" What would you say to them?

THE PURPOSE OF THIS BOOK

The purpose of this book is to reach out to those who haven't accepted Jesus as their Savior and to share the love God has for them. God loves us so much that He does not want anyone to perish. That is why He sent His Son to do for us what we were unable to do for ourselves. Everyone will have to choose to either accept what He came to do for you and enjoy the blessings of that, or try to get into heaven on your own and suffer the consequences that come with that.

Everyone will be held accountable for their own choices. The Bible is available for everyone to read, and it is easy to understand. Many people believe that if they live a good enough life they will go to heaven, but that is not what the Bible teaches.

Picture it this way: When you die, you will be standing in front of two doors. One door reads Old Testament (Under Law) and the other door reads

New Testament (Under Grace). So now you have to choose which of the two doors you want to go through. We know that everyone who enters through the law door will be judged by whether they kept all of the Ten Commandments. But, remember, you will be judged according to God's standard, and if you break one of the Ten Commandments you will be found guilty of breaking the whole law, which leads to death.

No one will be able to enter heaven through the law door because everybody is guilty of breaking the law, and that leads to death.

If you choose to enter through the grace door (grace means undeserving favor, but God gives it to you anyway), He will show mercy on you and allow you to enter His kingdom. For grace is given to all who believe in His Son Jesus, that He paid the price for all your sins on the cross.

Jesus came to this earth to do the will of His Father, which was to be a sacrifice for our sins. But before Jesus went to the cross, He pleaded with His Father three times to remove the cup of suffering He was about to endure. But He said "if there is no other way to save them, let your will be done." So you see, you will be considered righteous because of what Jesus did for you on the cross, and not because of how good you think you have lived your life.

That is why there is only one way to enter heaven, by trusting in His Son, Jesus.

My hope is that you can see the love the Father has for you. He sent His Son to pay the price for your sins so that you can be with Him in heaven. By putting your trust in His Son, you will be covered under the new covenant of grace, which the Father freely gives to you for believing in His Son. When you accept Jesus as your Savior, you are released from the law of the old covenant and are covered under the new covenant of grace.

This is truly amazing love—that a King would send His Son down from His throne to die for you. The Good News is that He *did* send His Son down here to the earth to shed His blood on a cross to cover your sins.

IT ALL COMES DOWN TO THIS

John 3:16-18

For **God so loved** the world that he gave his one and only Son, that **whoever believes** in him shall not perish but **have eternal life**.

For God **did not** send his Son into the world **to condemn** the world, **but to save** the world through him.

Whoever believes in him is not condemned, but **whoever does not believe** stands condemned already because he has not believed in the name of God's one and only Son.

BLESSED ASSURANCE

This book is written so that you can be assured of having eternal life in heaven with the Father and His Son. God loves you so much that He sent His Son down here to pay the penalty for all your sins. So you see, it is not about you or how good a life you can live. It is all about what God's Son has done for you already.

Now there is something you have to do to be assured of this eternal life in heaven.

You must be sincerely sorry for the sins you have committed. Then you have to accept God's Son (Jesus) as your Savior. That is, you must *believe* that because Jesus shed His blood, all your sins have been *and* will be forgiven. When you accept Him as your Savior, you are also accepting Him as your Lord. (Lord means *One having power and authority over others.)*That means you are willing to obey His commands, which are not burdensome.

They are:

- to love the Lord your God with all your heart, soul, mind, and strength.
- to love others and treat them the way you would want to be treated.
- to tell others about the Good News of the gospel so they too can be saved. I am not saying that you have to travel to a distant land to tell others about this Good News. But you should tell your family, your friends, and maybe your co-workers about what God has done for you so that they too can be with you in heaven.
- to be baptized in the name of the Father and the Son and the Holy Spirit.

Once you have accepted Jesus as your Savior, when you die you will be able to stand righteous before the Father, not because of anything you have done, but because of what His Son has done for you. 1 Peter 1:18-19 For you know that it was not with perishable things such as silver or gold that you were redeemed…, but with the precious blood of Christ, a lamb without blemish or defect. His blood was shed to cover all your sins, and the Father will have mercy on you for believing in His Son, granting you grace so that you can enter His heavenly kingdom.

1 John 5:13 "I write these things to you who believe in the name of the Son of God so that you may know that you have eternal life."

MY PRAYER FOR YOU

My prayer is that you accept that Jesus came and fulfilled the will of His Father, which was to shed His blood on the cross so that your sins would be forgiven. So please put your trust in Jesus and what He said He came here to do for you. Do not put your hope in your own works, or traditions, or anything else that you may be trying to do to get into heaven.

Jesus said, "I am the way, the truth, and the life, and no one can come to the Father except through me." By accepting Jesus as your Lord and Savior, your name will be written down in the Book of Life, and the Father will grant you eternal life! Jesus is the only way!

ARE YOU HEAVEN BOUND?

Everybody wants to go to heaven, but most people don't know how to get there. In the Bible, God tells us clearly what we must do to get there.

In John Chapter 6, we are told of a crowd that was following Jesus. He knew the reason they were following Him was because He fed them. Jesus told them, "…you shouldn't be so concerned about perishable things like food. Spend your energy seeking the eternal life that I, the Son of Man, can give you. For God the Father has sent me for that very purpose.

They replied, 'What does God want us to do?'

Jesus told them, 'This is what God wants you to do: Believe in the one he has sent.'" (John 6:27-29 NLT)

Jesus goes on to say in John 6:6 NLT, "It is the Spirit who gives eternal life. Human effort accomplishes nothing."

This shows us that we cannot do anything physically to obtain heaven. We have to have a spiritual understanding of God's plan. We have to believe in the reason He sent His son to earth and trust that it was enough to pay our way to heaven. If we accept His Son as payment and allow Him to guide our lives, He will take us to heaven—even though we make mistakes!!

MY INVITATION TO YOU

Today, if you are hearing God's voice speaking to you, don't ignore it. Open your heart and let Him come into your life; you will never regret it. What God has in store for those who love Him is far better than anything we can ever imagine.

Ask Jesus to come into your life and forgive you of your sins. Then obey His commands and find a Bible-teaching church to help you in your walk with the Lord.

Remember, God said He will never leave you or forsake you. He will be with you always.

You can accept Jesus as your Savior and be obedient to Him because you understand the love He has for you. Or you can accept Jesus as your Savior and be obedient to Him because you are afraid of going to hell and spending your eternity in the Lake of Fire. I know that once you come to know the love God has for you, you too will come to love the Lord.

Are you ready to accept Jesus as your Lord and Savior, or will you put it off and say "Maybe later...I have to think about it some more"? Well, that's the same as denying Him at this time. The problem with that is we don't know how much time we have to live here on this earth.

Tragic deaths happen to people of all ages. No one knows how long they will live. If you hear His voice calling today, don't put it off any longer. One day it will be too late.

If you would like to accept Jesus as your Savior right now, all you have to do is invite Him into your life, acknowledge that you have sinned, and let Him know that you are sincerely sorry for those sins. Tell Him that you accept His blood as payment for those sins and are willing to live the rest of your life trying to please Him.

If you are now ready to let God's Son come into your life, I ask you to repeat the prayer below.

Acceptance Prayer

Father, I know I have sinned, and I ask You now to forgive me of those sins. I thank You for sending Your

Son to pay for my sins, and I accept Your Son as my Lord and Savior.

1 John 5:13 "I write these things to you who believe in the name of the Son of God so that you may know that you have eternal life."

CPSIA information can be obtained at www.ICGtesting.com
Printed in the USA
LVOW041353060412

276454LV00001B/16/P